To The Hognack's Family,
May your dreams be as you turn [?] of this book

SHE DARES TO *Dream*

Psalm 37:4

Jan Tennyson

BY JAN TENNYSON

SHE DARES TO *Dream* —THE JAN TENNYSON STORY

Copyright © 2010 by Jan Tennyson
First Edition
Printed in the United States of America

This book was prepared for publication by:
Palm Tree Productions
Keller, Texas 76244 | *www.palmtreeproductions.net*

No part of this book may be used or reproduced in any manner whatsoever without written permission from the author. All rights reserved. International copyright secured.

Unless otherwise identified, Scripture quotations are from the New King James Version of the Bible. Copyright © 1982 by Thomas Nelson, Inc. Used by permission. All rights reserved.

Scripture quotations identified NIV are from the Holy Bible, New International Version®. NIV Copyright © 1973, 1978, 1984 by International Bible Society. Used by permission of Zondervan Publishing House. All rights reserved.

ISBN: 978-0-9826954-3-2

Library of Congress Control Number: 2010932473

To contact the author:

www.daretodream—dallas.org

"As a child who grew up in the foster care system in New York City, Jan shares stories of how, with 'holy boldness,' she approaches at-risk children's group homes, shelters, detention centers, and orphanages. Her point that God can use the power of your story to encourage others and direct you to your purpose in life comes through loud and clear. It's an inspring book, and one that will prompt you to step out and do more with your own life."

Zig Ziglar | Author/Motivational Speaker

"You have established an outstanding record of community service. I congratulate you on your achievements. Your efforts show that the values on which our nation was founded are still embedded in the American character. I commend you for helping to sustain our national tradition of neighbor-helping-neighbor and for making a positive difference in the life of your community."

Barbara and George Bush | Former President of the United States
The White House, Washington, D.C.

"What this old world needs is more people like you, encouraging kids to be all they can be while there is still time for them to mature into greatness and be motivated. Today we hear of so many children whose lives have been thrown into turmoil, both emotionally and physically, by abuse. I think it is wonderful that you are doing something about that in giving these children hope."

Mary Kay Ash | Founder, Mary Kay Cosmetics 1992

Dedication

*To my brothers and sisters who grew
up with me in our foster home.*

*To my children Lisa and James, their spouses David and Dana,
and my grandchildren Madeline, Robert, Samantha, and Lane.*

*To the wounded children of the world who have
been abused, neglected, and abandoned, and grew up in
orphanages, shelters, group homes, and foster care.*

Author, Jan Tennyson
Founder, Dare to Dream Children's Foundation

Acknowledgements

Marla Benroth and Helen Hosier—Your incredible talents and inspiration have been invaluable as you helped me put words to my memories.

To all who took their precious time, over the years, to read portions of this book, I am forever grateful— Ken & Barbie Cordier, Barbara Flyg, Patty Furr, Vicki Garza, Margaret Johnson, Jean Philp, Gretta Prosper, Pete & Sandy Riffe, Lynn Sinclair, Della Sowunmi, and Jann Trice.

Steve & Mary Vogds, and Richard & Barbara Flygg—I am thankful to you for providing your beautiful homes in Colorado to me as I purged my soul and put difficult words on paper.

Ann Platz—for your gracious hospitality and example of a grand southern lady who has enriched my life with love.

Todd & Wendy Walters—for your patience and commitment to excellence working with me as a first time author.

To those who have supported me with your talents, resources and prayers—you will remain in my heart with gratitude forever. This story couldn't been written without you.

Contents

Part One
My Collection of Hearts

- 21 **Introduction**
- 23 **One—Humble Beginnings**
  - *A Fragile Heart*—History Repeats Itself
  - *A Grateful Heart*—Helping Hands
  - *A Devoted Heart*—A Child and a Crown
  - *A Disappointed Heart*—"What do you expect from a Drunk?"
  - *A Determined Heart*—Showtime for the Pianist
  - *An Abandoned Heart*—The Curtain Came Down

- 43 **Two—The Good, the Bad, and the Ugly**
  - A Parade of Children
  - Precious Memories
  - School Days Rule Days
  - "No Business Like Show Business"
  - Christmas at the Foundling
  - Tragedy Hits Home
  - "I Want You to Be My Baby"
  - A Hardened Heart
  - Free at Last
  - Foster Parents of the Year
  - A Mission Field in the Making

- 67 **Three—Small Steps to Great Adventures**
  - Corporate America
  - Globe Trotting Adventures

79   FOUR—DREAM ON
- My Prince Charming
- A Family to Grow On
- Making it Work
- A Crumbling Castle

95   FIVE—DESTINY PLAYS A PART
- The Touch of a Mother's Hand
- A Memory to Last a Lifetime

105   SIX—LETTING GO
- Hearing the Silence
- It is Finished
- A Celebration and a Bedside Melody
- No Regrets

115   SEVEN—A SEARCH FOR MEANING
- Digging Family Roots
- Children Without Dreams

PART TWO
The Dare to Dream Story

125   INTRODUCTION

127   EIGHT—THE START OF SOMETHING BIG
- The Right Stuff
- Money from Heaven
- A Mother's Heart and a Soldier's Strength
- Focusing on the Dream
- Sharing the Dream
- The Dream Takes Wings
- My Last Call

149   Nine—The Children are Our Future
- Straight from the Kids
- An Evening with the Stars
- Shining Lights
- Triumph of the Human Spirit

163   Ten—Divine Appointments
- "The Sea Dream"
- A Christmas Boat Parade
- A Room at the Top
- Music on the Mountain
- Released from the Chains
- Ladies Choice
- A Party with a Purpose
- Flying High
- "The Best Years of Your Life" Contest

Part Three
My Spiritual Journey

197   Introduction

199   Eleven—My Transformation
- A Mission Field in he Making
- A Turning Point
- A Breaking Point
- An Earth Angel Bouquet
- The Jesus Video
- A Dream Come True
- The Great Commission
- A Miracle in Turkey
- The Army of God in Romania
- A Candle in Thailand
- A Banquet Table in Russia

233 TWELVE—WOW STORIES
- The Sound of Music
- A Rocket Ship to Heaven
- A Final Home Run
- One in a Million
- A Vision in the Clouds
- Think of a Rainbow
- My Gift from the Sea
- A Graveside Savior
- The Great Wall of China
- A Church in a Garbage Dump

PART FOUR
Leave a Living Legacy

253 THIRTEEN—THE BEST IS YET TO COME
- Amazing Grace
- The Power of the Written Word
- She Dares to Dream

261 ADDENDUM
- Testimonials
- Awards
- Volunteer and Donation Information
- Credits
- One Solitary Life

As you read this book, you will find the truth of this promise from our heavenly Father regarding seemingly impossible situations:

> ♥ *"… I will make a road in the wilderness*
> *and rivers in the desert "*
> (Isaiah 43:19).

Foreword

In speaking, I say, "Everyone has a story in them; our lives are stories—the past, the present, and the yet-to-be..." Not everyone's story gets written and published, but when I first heard Jan Tennyson speak, I knew this was a story worthy of publication and told her so. I encouraged her to begin writing it. Now look at what you hold in your hands! This is an investment readers will appreciate. You will be inspired and blessed.

The real power of Jan's story is how her strong faith comes through time after time; how she allows the Holy Spirit to take control as she confronts the multiple challenges that arise; and how she gives God the credit and praise throughout.

Through *She Dares to Dream* we see the tragedy of parental alcohol addiction and the heartache it brings into the lives of innocent children. We are given glimpses of the sadness of mental illness. But then we observe the determination of a young woman to overcome and rise above the forces that could have kept her a victim. Her resiliency and courage, the resolve that moved her to overcome, and then the faith she developed as she put her trust in Jesus, the One who made a way for her—it is all here in this powerful, moving account.

There is joy and excitement, miraculous intervention, adventuresome travels, a fearless spirit, faith in God's bigness, and the quiet humility of a gracious woman who loves God's children—young, in-between, or old—willing to do for others what God has done in her. Dream your own dreams, pursue your vision, and let the beauty of this book help and motivate you.

Helen K. Hosier

Helen is well known in the world of Christian communications as a writer and a speaker. She has sixty titles to her credit and is best known for *Cameos, Women Fashioned by God, Living the Lois Legacy* and *100 Christian Women who Changed the 21st Century*.

Preface

Many children who grew up in foster care have heartbreaking stories. Mine was just one of them. I'm writing about my life because I want to pass on what I have learned and want to encourage readers to know that there is light at the end of the tunnel of despair. Cruel experiences can break a life….but God can make a way when there seems to be no way. If just one person's faith can be strengthened through reading this book, then my purpose in writing it has been fulfilled.

The good, the bad, and the ugly events I've shared will make you laugh, cry, and wonder about the future of children growing up in very unpredictable circumstances. These children often wonder, Who am I? Who are my parents? Who is ever going to love me?

Because of the tragedy of family alcoholism and mental illness of a parent, I grew up in the foster care system in New York. As an adult, experiencing the devastation of divorce and the effects of substance abuse on a family, my life was in shambles. A never-give-up attitude to make life better for myself and my family propelled me into a life guided by the Holy Spirit to begin an organization that would build the self-esteem and spiritual values of abused, neglected, and foster children, many who become teen offenders and end up in prison.

Without a Heavenly Father who loved me at my worst, I could have ended up on the streets or in prison; but people of faith reached out to me and helped me to learn about the Bible, taught me how to pray, and held my hand and showed me how to walk with God.

My dream is that someone reading this book will be inspired to dream big dreams and know that with God all things are possible. Life is a lot better with Him than without Him. I believe sincerely that the best is yet to come—so I continue to *dare to dream*.

Part One

My Collection of Hearts

Gifts from the sea found by Jan Tennyson.

Introduction

"Let sleeping dogs lie!" That was the advice my three siblings echoed as I embarked on a pilgrimage to search for my roots. I ignored their advice. Having lived in foster care homes since infancy, I hungered for answers and was filled with questions about the unknown. Who were my parents and grandparents... and who was I? To find a trace of dignity in the ugly circumstances that surrounded the lives of my family became an obsession. The pain of change and crisis in our lives fueled my desire to help destitute and wounded children around the world. So, from the beginning, something good was being birthed from all the uncertainties. Still, the truth is the truth. I had a right to find it and my ancestors had a right to be remembered.

I was born in Greenwich Village, New York, in 1940. The world was in turmoil, and President Roosevelt warned our nation about *unpreparedness* in case of war. German troops paraded through Paris in a display of military might as a concentration camp was being built in Auschwitz. World events continued to escalate. Hitler captured Denmark and Norway; Churchill became Prime Minister; and the first U.S. military draft was drawn.

While many agonized over Europe's future, others *dared to dream* of wealth and prosperity. The British launched their luxury liner, the *Queen Elizabeth*. That same year, songwriters preferred to look on the positive side of life and penned such hits as "When You Wish Upon a Star," "How High the Moon," and "I Hear Music."

Little did I know that decades later, close to the place where I was born, the eyes of the world would be focused on an unprecedented event in the history of America—the invasion of a foreign power on our soil. President Roosevelt's prophetic warning about *unpreparedness* rang true for both my country and my family. Like the unsuspecting victims of the World Trade Center on September 11, 2001, our family was *unprepared* for one assault after another—poverty, lack of education, alcoholism, and mental illness. We too, crumbled and fell.

Chapter One

Humble Beginnings

One cold October morning in 1983, a blue Packard drove slowly through tall black wrought-iron gates onto the grounds of Rockland State Psychiatric Center. It followed the winding road, finally settling on a parking spot at the bottom of a hill. Two women dressed in heavy black coats emerged. Shivering, arm-in-arm, they walked on the pebbly ground as the orange and red autumn leaves swirled around them. Climbing to the top of the hill, breathing frost into the morning air, they stood before the wooden door of a small stone chapel. One of the women rang the door chime. A Catholic nun, dressed in a long black habit, opened the heavy door and nodded as they whispered introductions. She quietly escorted them through the church, past the empty pews to the back of the chapel where a small open casket sat on rollers in the vestibule. Holding hands, they moved closer, and then solemnly gazed at the small-framed body of a woman with graying blonde hair. She was dressed in a simple silk white blouse and pink jacket. This was the funeral of a patient who came to this institution when she was twenty-eight, lived on these grounds forty-three years, and died October 13, 1983, at the age of seventy-one. She was my mother.

Moments later, the nun asked my sister, Peggy, and me to take our seats, as the Mass was about to begin. I glanced around the chapel hoping to see some singers or someone playing the organ. There was no one. The silence was deafening. "Isn't there going to be any music?" I anxiously asked a nun nearby.

The sister apologized. "I'm sorry, but this is a small funeral, and we don't have anyone to play the organ."

"Could I play?" I quickly asked. With a surprised look on her face, she smiled and nodded. Then two elderly nuns kindly offered to sing. Instantly, I turned towards the staircase and ran up the creaky, wooden steps to the choir loft, discovering a dusty run-down relic that probably hadn't been played in decades. Frantically opening the bench searching for sheet music, I found none. Undaunted, I dusted off the keys and began playing Catholic hymns from memory before the service began.

Peering over the ledge of the choir loft, I gazed at the small brown coffin, now closed, being rolled down the center aisle to the front of the church. There was a beautiful spray of red roses placed on top—the only flowers in the church. I watched my sister walk slowly down the aisle and solemnly take her seat to the left of the casket. A handful of people sprinkled here and there filled the pews, quietly waiting. Teardrops ran down my face as I placed my fingers on the keys and began to softly play "Amazing Grace." The elderly nuns took their cue and lifted their shaky voices in song. Two altar boys with the Monsignor walked into the sanctuary, and the Mass began. He said a few words, served Communion, and the service was over. As the attendees trickled out of the chapel, a staff member escorted Peggy and me to the kitchen area for some refreshments and to visit with a few of our mother's aides and two of the nuns.

"When she was on medication, she was a happy friendly person," said one of the nurses. "We all loved her and will miss her," another aide told me.

I said, "I couldn't visit her often, but it gives me comfort knowing that you cared and enjoyed being with her."

Humble Beginnings

We left the building and followed the staff member's car past a sign that pointed to the Catholic section of Blaisdell Road Cemetery just outside the gates of the institution. Standing at the open grave shivering in the frosty air, Peggy and I placed a bright red rose on the small coffin. Choking back the tears, we murmured a prayer and walked slowly through the leaves back to our car.

I was sad, but thankful that I could give my simple gift of music. How perfect that heaven orchestrated this moment for a daughter—separated from a mother for so many years—to have the honor of bringing music to the final memory of her earthly presence.

A Fragile Heart...
History Repeats Itself

For years I carried with me the myth that my father left me at the New York Foundling Home because my mother had a nervous breakdown, and he was incapable of caring for me. But the truth is, my parents were alcoholics; my mother was mentally ill; and we children were being neglected. Consequently, the police took us away from our parents. Growing up in an orphanage himself and deprived of a loving family upbringing, my father did not have examples of how to raise his own children.

My brother Joe still remembers when he was eight, along with his four-year-old sister Peggy, wandering the docks of New York City at night asking desperately, "Have you seen our dad?" (Joe knew that's where Dad would line up in the morning along the waterfront with other men. All were hoping to be chosen to work as a longshoreman loading crates on tankers.) That night in 1940, the police saw my two ragged-looking lost siblings walking hand in hand on the waterfront and asked them where they lived. Joe told the officer, and somehow the police located Dad. Eventually, he picked them up from the station, angry they had left the small apartment in the tenements on 24th Street where we lived.

In October that same year, both our parents, within a week of each other, were transported by ambulance to Bellevue Hospital for intoxication. A neighbor informed the police that Mom was drunk and neglecting us. The police put Joe and Peggy in a children's shelter, and because I was only three months old, I went directly to the New York Foundling Home. It was run by Catholic Charities for homeless children under the age of two. At the shelter, Joe recalls looking out a two-story window into a rain-slick street wondering *When is Dad ever going to come and get me?* But he never did. A few weeks later, Joe and Peggy were court ordered into the custody of the Foundling Home and then placed in foster care.

My dad, Joseph Lowery and brother, Joe

Alcoholism led my mother to have a nervous breakdown when she was twenty-eight, which eventually caused her to be admitted to the Rockland State Psychiatric Center in Orangeburg, New York. Built to relieve overcrowding in city hospitals, the Institution opened in 1931 with a capacity of five thousand patients; by 1953, nine thousand and seven hundred patients lived on these grounds.

My mom, Florence Lowery and brother, Joe

From time to time Mom improved and went home with Dad. On one such visit, she got pregnant with Gene; however, shortly afterwards, she relapsed and went back to the Rockland State Institution, where she spent the rest of her life. Gene was placed in the Foundling Home. Now, all four of the Lowery children were officially integrated into the social service system in New York City.

A Grateful Heart
Helping Hands

A childless couple in their mid-forties opened their hearts and home to my siblings, Joe and Peggy. Charlie and Lucy Brennan had hoped to have a family of their own long before my sister and brother came on the scene. That dream seemed shattered when they found out Lucy couldn't have biological children. So, they applied to the Foundling Home and were approved as foster parents.

Charlie, a stocky Irishman, who stood at five foot seven with dark black hair, had a big heart and loved children. His sense of humor kept smiles on our faces. As the dedicated breadwinner in the family, he worked for thirty years at Fahnstock & Company, a brokerage firm in the Wall Street area.

His wife, Lucy, hailed from French-German ancestry. She was five feet tall, slightly plump, with lovely light blue eyes and a dewy complexion. Her appearance was a startling display of contrasts. She never wore makeup, and her skin was as clear and fresh as a young college girl. Yet, since her early thirties, her hair was as white as snow. In her younger years, she was a registered practical nurse and caretaker.

Joe and Peggy were separated from one another at first but were fortunate to eventually be placed together with the Brennans. Many times, siblings are placed in different homes and never get to know one another.

After living for three months as an infant in the Foundling Home, a loving couple living in Brooklyn, Walter and Edith Cochran, opened their foster home and cared for me as if I were their own. To celebrate my second birthday, they wrote the Brennans and kindly invited my brother and sister to come to my party. For reasons I do not know, Lucy did not respond to their invitation.

Since one of the primary goals of the Foundling was to keep siblings together, in 1942, when I was two and a half, they removed me from the Cochran's and placed me with the Brennans. I became their third foster child. As hard as it was for the Cochrans to let me go, they wanted what was best for the little girl they had grown to love. Being uprooted from my biological mother as an infant, and again being separated from loving foster parents, was traumatic on a little baby. As young as I was, the Cochrans tried to keep in touch and wrote letters to me at the Brennans. I can still remember the striking penmanship of Uncle Walter—the name he gave himself once I left his home.

When I was five years old, Edith Cochran died and her family invited me to attend the wake. Though I was just a little girl, I remember the event clearly. Wearing a pale blue organdy dress sprinkled with polka dots at the funeral parlor, I gazed at my first foster mother in her casket and wanted her to wake up and tell me she loved me just one more time. She looked like a large porcelain doll sleeping quietly in her bed. Even at that young age, I knew when I was loved, and I had truly felt loved by Edith and Walter Cochran.

God must have been watching me as an infant abandoned in a Greenwich Village apartment, and placed me in the New York Foundling Home. Then he opened the door to a couple who shared genuine love during the most important first years of my life.

A Devoted Heart

A Child and a Crown

As a six year old about to enter grammar school, I had to take a reading readiness test given by the Catholic Charities Guidance Institute of the Archdiocese of New York. The record read:

She appeared to the examiner as a rather frail-looking little girl, tending toward quietness. Her appearance shows good physical care. She was friendly, but she was not free and wholly at ease. On the basis of this examination, it appears that Janice should make satisfactory adjustment in first grade. This was discussed with the boarding mother, whose talkative manner seemed to overpower Janice. She had been giving Janice piano lessons and teaching her at home. She said that Janice wants to be a music teacher and schoolteacher, and she thinks it is good to start children young. Although the child is undoubtedly capable, it would be well to guard against the boarding mother applying too many pressures.

The examiner was right. Guarding every word that came out of my mouth and being told by my foster mother that I'd be kicked out if one wrong word was spoken made me very uneasy. So, yes, I was quiet and seldom said much about anything.

Ever since I was little, it seems like God was tugging at my heart. I looked forward to the month of May when the Catholic Church honored Mary, who was a symbol of a mother who loved me no matter what. Families built small altars in their homes as a tribute to the Blessed Virgin. The fragrance of pink roses from our garden filled the room as we prayed the rosary around her statue each evening.

When I was six, a small basket with blank pieces of paper was passed around to the girls in my classroom. Only one piece had the name of *Mary* written on it. Anxiously, we sat on the edge of our seats wondering, *Who will crown Mary in church this year?* I picked her name!

Wearing the gorgeous white dress and veil my foster mother bought me for the celebration, I shuffled up to the front of the line as my classmates stood in single file in the hallway. With everyone staring at me, I felt nervous as I slowly led the procession down the center aisle of the church carrying a crown of small white roses. As I approached the foot of the magnificent statue, the congregation sang "O Mary We Crown Thee With Blossoms Today." Standing on my tiptoes, I reached up high and placed the fragrant crown on her head.

First Communion Day 1946

Reflecting on the service as I walked across the street to our home, I felt like I had been halfway to heaven. But my glow didn't last very long.

The next day, my foster mother shouted, "Finish your breakfast!" She glared at me as I tried to stuff spoonfuls of cereal into my mouth. My stomach felt like it was going to explode, but she insisted I finish every drop. The kids around the breakfast table watched and fidgeted, knowing full well that Joe and I could not leave for school until my bowl was empty. Because of me, we were going to be late again. Finally, I managed to get the last bite down as we scrambled out the door and briskly walked ten blocks to The Immaculate Conception School in Brooklyn. Embarrassed, I quickly took my seat at the end of the third row of wooden desks and was relieved when Sister Marion didn't make my late arrival an issue in front of the students.

Suddenly, the door to my classroom opened and a volunteer handed my teacher a note. My heart pounded as I heard my name being called and was told to follow the volunteer to my brother's classroom. I obediently got up and walked out of the room, sensing the stares of my peers on the back of my neck. The messenger, older than me and pretty with curly blonde hair, spoke comforting words that did little to ease my nervousness. We walked down the long hallway past the cafeteria and arrived at Joe's classroom. Reluctantly, I walked through the door the girl held open and into the class of gawking eighth graders. Joe's teacher looked up, frowned and began interrogating me.

"Why is your brother always late? He says it is because of you."

Wishing the floor would open up and swallow me, I looked down as my eyes filled with tears. "I'm sorry," I stammered. "I try to eat as fast as everyone else in the morning, but I can't…" I shyly stole a glance at the teacher, who was frowning at me, her lips pursed. I gulped and continued weakly, "My brother had to wait for me to finish my breakfast."

"Very well then," she said with a stern voice. "Then you will do this homework assignment: write *I will not be late again*—fifty times! And bring it back to me." My shoulders slumped as I walked towards the door to return to my classroom. This nun seemed like anything but a Sister of Mercy. In a few months, our family was going to move from Brooklyn to Bayside. I looked forward to moving more than anyone knew.

A Disappointed Heart...
"What Do You Expect from a Drunk?"

Since we had a mom who was incapable of mothering us, our visits with our dad became very important moments. One Saturday morning, waiting all dressed up and sitting on the black tweed couch in our living room, Joe and Peggy anxiously peered through the curtain for a cab that would bring our Dad to take us on an outing to New York City. I was seven; Gene was five and too young to join us at the time.

"Is he here yet?" I asked.

Peggy said, "Not yet...oh, wait!" She pushed the curtains back further. A taxi pulled to the curb and she shouted, "There he is!" The doorbell rang, and we all sprang to answer it. It was our dad, tall and handsome with brown wavy hair. He had hugs for each of us, but as his reddened face leaned close to mine, I smelled an unfamiliar odor on his breath.

"We're going to Radio City," he announced, to our squeals of delight. Loving music and dance productions, he took us to either Radio City Music Hall or the famous Roxy Theatre. Waving goodbye to our foster parents standing on the stoop, we climbed into the taxi and drove off to our exciting day in the Big Apple.

Arriving at the Long Island Railroad's Pennsylvania Station in Manhattan, we paraded with Dad through the crowded terminal passing specialty stores, restaurants with their inviting aromas, and kiosks where local folks sold their crafts. We tried to walk hand in hand, not losing one another as we wound around the sidewalks, squeezing between the bodies, down the stairs into the hole in the ground to the train. We then rushed to the ticket counter to purchase our fares. Dad handed my two older siblings ten-cent tokens to deposit in the metal box, but because I was so little, he told me to duck underneath. Standing on the platform, we watched expectantly for the train which eventually rolled into the station and slowly came to a halt in front of us. After riding to our next stop in the crowded compartment, we piled out and walked two blocks to the famous Music Hall.

Entering the expansive foyer with plush red-carpeted staircases spiraling down on each side, I paused silently in awe of the magnificent shimmering crystal chandeliers. Making our way up the huge staircase to our seats in the half-moon shaped balcony, I turned to see where the music was coming from. Lively tunes chimed out from a white organ on the small balcony to the left of the stage as the entertainer played "Give My Regards to Broadway."

Humble Beginnings

Excitement was high as the lights dimmed, and a spotlight focused on the announcer welcoming the crowd. Applause filled the theatre as Ginger Rogers, in her sheer long flowing evening gown, and Fred Astaire, in his black tuxedo, gracefully waltzed across the movie screen. It was so entertaining that I wanted to jump out of my seat and dance! I could tell Dad was thoroughly enjoying every moment, as he would peer across the aisle from time to time smiling at us.

At intermission, we hurried down the staircase lining up for our treats. Sipping sodas and eating ice cream bonbons was interrupted as Dad announced we needed some fresh air. Actually, it was for his cigarette break. Ten minutes later, as the lights blinked, we climbed the tall staircase back to our seats. We arrived just in time for the live stage show. Trumpets blasted a toe-tapping introduction as the giant red velvet curtain opened and dozens of long-legged beauties kicked their way across the stage. The famous Rockettes, with their sparkly red costumes and precision movements, dazzled the crowd. At that moment, I knew I wanted to be a dancer. As the last act exited and the audience stood to its feet roaring with applause, I stood on my tiptoes to get a last look at the stage. Then we followed the swarming crowds out of the theatre.

Stepping onto the train, Dad nudged me and said, "Let's grab some food at the Bayside Diner." "Yea!" we all shouted with glee. It was one of our favorite places to eat. The Diner was an old-timey relic, complete with twelve bar stools and booths with bright red plastic seats. A small jukebox was sitting against the wall on each table. Hurrying to an empty booth in the diner crowded with locals, yummy smells of mashed potatoes, gravy, and fresh veggies filled the air. We slid in, two on each side.

"Can I have a dime?" Peggy asked, pointing to the jukebox. Dad gladly dug a coin out of his pocket and she popped it into the slot. She chose Elvis' romantic melody "Love Me Tender" and the Everly Brothers' "Blueberry Hill." The waitress, dressed in a black-and-white pinafore, stepped to the table, pen poised, to take our order. Dad joked, "Hello sweetheart, it's nice of you to have us over for dinner."

"I slaved all day just waiting for you guys to arrive," the waitress responded with a wink.

Having a fun time with our dad was a real treat, and sometimes I wished he would take us to his home, but he never did. The waitress brought our food, and as I hastily picked up my fork, gravy dribbled from my chin to my blue dress. Dad, who was shaking salt on his meal like a crop duster, quickly reached across the table with a smile and gently dabbed my face and dress with a napkin. Surprised, but grateful, I waited as he wiped it dry. It was getting late, so he hailed the waitress, who hurried to our table.

"What's the damage, chief?" he asked. Smiling, she scribbled on her pad, tore off the page and handed it to him. He paid the bill and called a taxi.

We got home and went inside where he hugged each of us and promised to come back soon. Turning to our foster parents, he said, "I can't thank you enough for taking such good care of my children."

"You're welcome; we love them too," my foster mom said, fondly looking at each of us.

Walking out the front door down the steps into the waiting taxi, he turned looking out the rear view window and smiled at us one more time. Peggy, Joe, and I stood outside our three-story house waving like crazy, as only kids will do, as the cab drove out of sight. Not knowing when we would see him again I wondered, *Where does he live? What kind of a life does he have?*

Dad's visits were important to us, but many times he disappointed us. One Saturday, dressed and ready to go, sitting on the couch, fidgeting, we waited and waited. Peggy ran to the window several times wondering, *Where is he? Did he forget us?*

Joe tried to reassure us. "Don't worry, he'll be here soon." When we realized that he was not coming, we were terribly upset.

"Well, what do you expect from a drunk?" our foster mother yelled sharply. Her judgmental words cut like a knife. She made me mad, but I bit my tongue not saying a word. Like most children, I loved my dad in spite of his problems and was hurt when bad things were said about him.

A Determined Heart

Showtime For the Pianist

As a young woman, my foster mother took piano lessons from Mr. Bergbrede, Director of the Brooklyn Conservatory of Music. Believing that children should start to learn at a young age, she generously offered each of us piano lessons. My brother and sister were not interested, but I was. So, when I turned six, she made an appointment for me to meet Mr. Bergbrede. I listened carefully as he presented a series of exercises on the black Baldwin baby grand on the stage. Delighted that I had perfect pitch, he was impressed with my potential.

"Janice, I'd love to have you as a student at this conservatory."

From then on, my foster mother had big plans for me—that I would become a well-known concert pianist. Little did I know that when I was accepted into the conservatory, it would be a major commitment on my part. My foster mother insisted that I practice three hours a day, like it or not.

Sitting on the piano bench in our living room, completely bored, playing scales and arpeggios over and over, my foster mother listened to every note from the kitchen. Hoping I wouldn't get caught, every now and then I'd peek out the window watching the kids having fun jumping rope or playing tag, resenting the fact that I could not join them.

Showing me off every chance they got, neighbors and friends stopped by, and I was asked to play my newest and most flashy piece of music. I dreaded being on display and fussed over.

My piano teacher, chosen by Mr. Bergbrede, was a strict, demanding woman, and if I didn't hold my hands a certain way over the keys, she would strike my knuckles with a ruler. It reminded me of when the nuns at Sacred Heart School slapped the palms of my hands with a ruler if I did something they didn't like. This seemed more like punishment than a piano lesson.

One of my teacher's pet peeves was the awkward way I walked. She said I looked like Charlie Chaplain, who walked with his heels together and his toes pointed out. Marching up and down the rehearsal room, practicing the *correct* way to walk was sheer agony. I now realize that she had my best interest at heart and was grooming me for the concert stage.

When I was seven, I was glad our family moved from Brooklyn to Bayside, Queens, to a large, three-story home with twelve rooms and a front porch with dozens of paned windows. Joe, Peggy and Gene spent hours making those windows sparkle. I didn't have to wash windows—nor anything else. My foster mother did not want me to ruin my piano hands. Watching me get dressed up for concerts, being eliminated from having to do dishes, and most of all, having to ride forty-five minutes with me to my mid-week piano lessons, caused a lot of resentment towards me from my siblings. My foster mother did not trust them to stay home alone, and I could not do anything about it.

Besides my weekly piano lessons, I attended theory and harmony classes at the conservatory on Saturdays. The best part was riding the Long Island Railroad into the city with my foster dad. He read the newspaper as I peered out the window

Humble Beginnings

passing houses, trees, and trains until we reached the tunnel that took us underground. After my morning classes, feasting at Dad's favorite restaurant for lunch was a real treat. While sipping on a cocktail as he enjoyed London broil, he'd reach over to pat my hand saying endearingly, "Janie, I'm so proud of you." I felt very special holding my daddy's hand as we walked out of the restaurant, returning to the conservatory. Dad sat in the audience smiling as I performed at the afternoon concert. Then we headed for our long journey home.

On one Saturday trip to the city, my foster dad recognized the famous radio and TV announcer, Ed Herlihy, on the train. He was the broadcaster for *The Horn and Hardart's Children's Hour*—a variety show with a cast of children, including some who later became well-known adult performers. It had a long run for more than three decades. The program was sponsored by Horn & Hardart, which owned restaurants, bakeshops and automats—a place to get fresh food from a vending machine in New York and Philadelphia. Dad was proud of me and told Mr. Herlihy about my concerts at the Brooklyn Conservatory of Music. He was impressed, but not much happened as a result of our meeting.

When I was almost eight, the conservatory held its final concert of the semester at Carnegie Hall in New York City. Waiting nervously in the wings for my turn to perform, the applause began to subside. It was my turn! Taking a deep breath, I told myself, *Be calm. You can do it.*

The conservatory director followed me as I walked across the expansive stage to the grand piano. Picking me up like a small doll, he placed me on the piano stool and left the stage. Trying to focus on remembering the notes and not being distracted by the hall filled to capacity with everyone staring at me, I placed my fingers on the keys and began to play the first of three of Bach's Fugues. My tiny hands ran across the keys as the musical themes repeated themselves, each one slightly different. Relieved, after hitting the last note, I carefully jumped off the stool and curtsied to the audience. The lengthy standing ovation made my heart sing! I did it! They loved it!

As I started to leave the stage with the people still clapping, a man ran down the center aisle carrying an enormous basket of multicolored flowers—the handle taller than me—and placed them on the stage smiling. I wondered, *Who sent these gorgeous flowers?* Mr. Bergbrede walked out on the stage to carry the basket and escort me to the wings. Later I found out they were from my proud foster parents.

At the reception after the concert, people greeted me with enthusiastic accolades.

"Janice, you were wonderful!"

"What an amazing performance!"

I was uncomfortable with the compliments and shyly turned away, not knowing how to respond. *Why didn't someone teach me to smile and just say thank you?*

After the festivities, I walked into our house still on a high from all the praise, but was quickly brought down to earth by the sarcastic remarks from my brother Joe. "How's the princess? Are you going to peel some potatoes now?" I acted like his cutting words didn't bother me, but they did. Nevertheless, with a resilient showbiz spirit, I quickly bounced back and didn't attempt to justify my whereabouts. I just continued to practice, practice, and practice.

When I was nine, the Foundling Home invited me to perform on a radio program to raise funds for Catholic Charities. Ted Mack, a famous host of his own TV show, *The Original Amateur Hour*, was the Master of Ceremonies. Some struggling amateurs who got their start on his show included Frank Sinatra, Pat Boone, Gladys Knight, Ann-Margret, Beverly Sills, Connie Francis, Maria Callas, Joey Dee and The Starlighters, and Robert Merrill.

I had no idea at the time how famous this man was when I was invited to the show. It was my turn to perform. Walking over to the baby grand, I sat down and confidently ran my fingers across the keys playing "Rondo" by Mozart. At the end of the performance, with a big smile, Mr. Mack remarked, "Janice, if you continue practicing and playing the piano like you did today, one day people will be hearing you all over the country. Your accomplishments, young lady, are noteworthy of an adult."

Looking up at him from the piano bench, I shyly replied, "Thank you, Mr. Mack."

Ted Mack and Ed Herlihy, two giants in the world of children's talent were put in my path at such a young age. What an incredible opportunity I might have had if someone had kept these relationships alive. Most parents would jump through hoops just to get in front of these celebrities. But, as is still true today, unless someone connects with the foster child to help them achieve their dreams, many may not reach their potential.

An Abandoned Heart
The Curtain Came Down

On several occassions, my foster mother would say, "I'm not your real mother, but someday you'll have an opportunity to meet her." In October, 1950, that day arrived.

Gene and I huddled together in the back seat of our old blue Packard while Peggy sat up front with our foster mother. Peering through the window, we saw the stately wrought-iron gates of Rockland State Psychiatric Center looming in the distance, accented against a crisp blue autumn sky. As we got closer, a dark-uniformed guard greeted us and gave my foster mother directions to the building where our mother lived. The gates opened slowly, and we wound around the campus past three-story red brick buildings and carefully coiffured grounds to a parking spot near her residence. I hesitantly got out of the car wondering, *What will she look like? Will she know me?* Buttoning my coat and taking a deep breath, I took my foster mother's hand as the four of us walked toward one of the buildings.

I was ten years old and minutes away from meeting my real mom for the first time since social services had removed me from our apartment as an infant. Knowing what it was like to be standing in the wings of a concert hall with my heart thumping and my palms sweating was difficult for me. But this was different. We were about to meet our biological mother and didn't know anything about her. Nor did anyone prepare us for what we were about to encounter. Noticing a short, stocky woman sitting on a park bench in the distance, we walked closer. A tall nurse in a starched white uniform stood beside her.

My foster mother greeted the nurse and said, "These are Florence's children." Standing silently at attention like cadets meeting a General for the first time, I stared at this woman who had light blue eyes and graying blonde hair, hoping she'd say something nice.

"Florence..." the nurse gently said to my mother, who was looking away, oblivious to her arriving guests, "These are your children, and this is your daughter, Janice."

She turned and looked at me for a moment and with a harsh voice said, "I don't care who that G_d d_mn kid is. Get me a cigarette!" With a piercing look from her weary blue eyes, she quickly shifted her focus away from me. Frightened by her uncaring attitude, I took a step backward, wounded by her outburst. My foster mother grabbed my hand and said, "Come on, let's go," hastily leading Peggy, Gene and me back to the car.

Humble Beginnings

As we drove off the grounds I thought, *A normal mommy wouldn't say that to her little girl.* Being unprepared to meet our mother and hearing her harsh words to me that day, I put up a wall that would shield my heart. From that day forward, I told anyone who asked about my family, "My parents were killed in a plane crash." I erased the truth from my thoughts.

When I was fourteen, our foster mother approached us with some shocking news. Our dad had been found dead in bed with two broken legs. Years later, The Foundling said they had no record of that report. Conflicting stories were confusing, and seldom did anyone sit down to clarify the facts for us. Without consolation or counseling, we had to stuff our feelings and our grief.

Standing in front of Dad's open grave in the rain at St. James Cemetery, across the river from Manhattan, is a vague memory. There were a handful of people dressed in black, most of whom I didn't know. My oldest brother Joe, on military leave from the aircraft carrier The USS *Ticonderoga* and looking handsome wearing his white Navy uniform, was sad as the priest said a prayer. Joe knew Dad longer than any of us and had a heavy heart. Feeling a pang of sadness, mixed with regret, I stared at the pauper's coffin that encased my dad's body, suspended over the open hole in the ground. I didn't know him well, but I would miss the little I did know—his laughter, our outings to Manhattan, and the few family meals we enjoyed at the Bayside Diner.

My fragile siblings and I already had low self-esteem, and with our mother locked in an institution and our dad gone, the only family we knew—the Brennans—would shape our destiny.

CHAPTER TWO

THE GOOD, THE BAD AND THE UGLY

A Parade of Children

A smorgasbord of children, six to eight at a time from a wide variety of ethnic backgrounds, filled the Brennan breakfast table for over two-and-a-half decades. Irish, German, Italian, Puerto Rican, and other nationalities each had their diverse stories of abandonment, neglect, poverty, or temporary displacement. My siblings, Joe and Peggy, were the first two placed in the Brennan's foster home in 1940; I arrived two-and-a-half years later. Rose, who we called Cookie, a cute two year old with blonde curly hair, came to live with us a year-and-a-half after me, and because of

Cookie, Peggy, Barbara, Joe, Jan, and Gene (front)

her sickly nature, the Brennans seemed to treat her as their favorite. My brother Gene, a sweet child, Joan, and other youngsters came later.

Gracie, a pretty Italian baby with brown curly hair, stayed with us until she was twelve; Kenneth, a handsome blonde, spent a year at our home and then was adopted by new parents. Frances, a mentally-challenged boy, stayed two years and eventually was placed in an institution where he could receive special education. The stories of the children were as diverse as the colors of the rainbow. The child who stayed the longest was Louis, a Puerto Rican baby, who grew up in our household and lived with us through adulthood. He cared for our foster parents as they grew into old age.

The Brennans also opened their arms to physically-challenged children like Barbara who had cerebral palsy and Ingrid with Down syndrome. Over the years, there were twenty-three youngsters in all with two to three toddlers at a time. Nationality or physical disability didn't matter; we loved each other as one big family—or so it seemed.

Precious Memories

Christmas was (and still is) my favorite time of year. Our foster parents went all out to make it a spectacular holiday for all of us. Venturing out with Dad the night before Christmas Eve, all bundled up with hat, coat, scarf, and gloves in the cold night air, searching from lot to lot for the tallest, most beautifully-shaped tree was a fun evening.

On Christmas Eve, after the children went to bed, helping Dad put twinkle lights on our *perfect* tree made me feel special. Handing him colorful ornaments, one by one, and watching him decorate the top part of the tree, as he stood on the ladder, was real teamwork. After the tinsel had been placed as straight as an arrow on each branch, Dad reached up and put the beautiful, shining star on top. He flipped the switch, and we stood hand in hand in silence admiring what looked as spectacular as any tree that you might see in the window of Macy's department store. Kissing each other goodnight, I hurried up to my room and snuggled under the covers so excited that I could hardly fall asleep that night.

Gene, Cookie, Louis, and Gracie

Dawn had broken as we fidgeted in our beds waiting for the signal to come downstairs. Standing in the hallway, Dad yelled with a cheery voice, "Merry Christmas everyone!" Scrambling, trying to line up on the staircase with the youngest in front and the oldest at the rear, we dashed downstairs trying not to tumble over one another running into the living room. Beneath the tree and throughout the room were Christmas presents piled so high that they spilled over into the next room. Our faces lit up as our foster parents, with happy eyes, passed out presents to each of us—quite a sight for a childless couple with a dream to have a family of their own.

One of our favorite activities was getting our clan together and heading to Coney Island, a famous amusement park in Brooklyn. We looked forward to the beach, the boardwalk, the rides, and the hot dogs. We could hardly wait to get there.

Piling out of the car and gazing up at the gigantic roller coaster, the most famous attraction in all of Coney Island, made me wonder if I would ever have the courage to ride it. Our walks on the boardwalk past advertisements for freak shows was a little scary, but with a hot dog in one hand and a balloon in the other, we quickly left that area and headed towards the sound of carnival music coming from the famous Feltman's merry-go-round. As we approached the ride, with its colorful painted horses, one by one we climbed on their backs and held on for dear life begging to ride a second time. And sometimes we did. Waving at the Brennans from the bumper cars and the loop-de-loop made me believe that they were having as much fun as we were. They stood on the sidelines watching us have a ball. My favorite time at Coney Island was staying until it got dark to see the colorful blinking lights and the excitement along the midway.

I have often wondered how my foster parents had enough eyes to watch eight children running from ride to ride and not losing any of us. Exhausted, some of the children fell asleep in the car on the way home. A great time was had by all!

School Days, Rule Days

Although I had a hard time eating in the morning and sometimes got to school late, tardiness was not the worst problem reported in school during those otherwise idyllic 1940s and 1950s. Talking out of turn, cutting in line, chewing gum, littering, making noise, shooting paper wads and running in the hallways were a few of the offenses. Some of the more rebellious kids would get in trouble for smoking cigarettes in the bathrooms. I don't ever recall hearing about suicide, abortions, or Satanism. Finding guns or knives in a student's locker were the last things one could ever imagine.

Our life at home was quite simple. After our homework, we played board games and listened to the radio. But when a neighbor down the block invited us to watch their black-and-white TV, we could hardly wait to watch *Hopalong Cassidy* and *Flash Gordon*. Eventually, we got our own television. Some of our favorites were *The Ed Sullivan Show, The Colgate*

Comedy Hour, Gunsmoke, Uncle Miltie, Rin Tin Tin, Lassie and *I Love Lucy*. Back then, shows were family friendly, and we didn't have to worry about viewing sex, violence, or hearing foul language.

With as many as ten mouths to feed in our home, grocery shopping was quite a task. Sometimes one or two of us were invited to go. Our treat was to stop by Smitty's Ice Cream parlor for a soda or a banana split before we returned home. But one day, when I was eight, our foster mom surprised us and went to the store by herself. She left us alone to be on our best behavior, which included no running in the house. As I practiced my lesson at the piano, Joe and Peggy came flying around the corner of the living room, passing me as they ran into the hallway. I held my breath; they knew this was wrong. But as a younger sibling, I did not dare recite any rules to them.

My foster mom came home shortly afterward with an armload of groceries. After putting them away, she smiled, took my hand and led me into the parlor. Picking me up and sitting me on her lap with her arm around my shoulder, she spoke in a smooth voice while coaxing me to tell her what went on with the other children during her absence. She told me that I would be helping them and asked, "You wouldn't want anything bad to happen to them while I'm gone, would you?" She gently patted my back as I squirmed, uncomfortable with her question.

We were taught to tell the truth; however, squealing on my own brothers and sisters did not seem right. I wanted to run but didn't dare. There was no way to win, and eventually, she manipulated me into being the informer.

Joe, grounded from playing baseball, yelled at me, "You little tattle-taler!" He threatened me with his fist and wanted to punch me out, but he didn't dare. "Mommy's little angel," he sneered. Humiliated, I tried to hold back my tears. These love-hate emotions wounded my tender heart and caused me to become a quiet, shy little girl who was afraid to speak up for herself.

"No Business Like Show Business"—

As an eight year old, I enjoyed watching shows with singing and dancing in the movies and on television. So, when I wasn't busy practicing piano, I became director of my own productions. I would invite boys and girls on my block to perform on my "stage on the stoop." The five long red brick steps that led up to the front door of our house were perfect for dance routines. The movie and stage productions at Radio City Music Hall were my inspiration.

Since we weren't allowed to have many interactions with school friends, the neighbor children on our block became the performers. Singers, dancers, readers, and joke tellers stood in line for auditions, and nobody was left out. I peered into the faces of the eager youngsters asking questions that would help me identify their talents.

"What are you good at?"

"Can you tap dance?"

"How about reading a poem?"

"If you don't want to perform, you can be part of the audience." The shows were a blast! Singing their hearts out and dancing like they were movie stars made me feel like we could have our own TV show.

This *show business* reputation got around. One day when I was nine, Father Ryan, one of the priests at Sacred Heart parish, invited me to visit his office. It was located in the same building as Sacred Heart School. Knocking on the door, I wondered what he wanted to speak to me about. The slim, red-haired priest opened the door and invited me to take a seat in a leather chair across from his desk. Sitting down, I gazed at the volumes of books covering the tall wooden shelves surrounding the room.

"Janice, I understand that you play the piano and like to dance."

"Yes I do, Father Ryan."

"Then, would you like to help me with the spring show for the parents of our school children?"

Without knowing what that entailed, I said *yes*. The day of the show arrived, and I have to admit I was a little nervous as I peeked through the curtains at my classmates sitting with their parents. Every seat in our school auditorium was filled.

Father Ryan welcomed the audience and then announced, "Let the show begin!" The curtain slowly opened as my younger brother, Gene, my foster sister, Cookie, and I stepped forward in our plaid outfits dancing the "Highland Fling" and the "Hopscotch Polka." Later in the show, dressed in a bright yellow satin jumper covered with large multi-colored polka dots, Gene rolled across the stage and performed a routine as an acrobatic clown. Small children singing, "How Much is that Doggie in the Window" touched a lot of hearts that day. And for the finale, I played "Rondo" by Mozart. My face reddened as the audience gave a standing ovation.

Father Ryan then announced to the audience—"I whispered one word in the ear of one little girl, and she accepted the challenge. We thank you so much, Janice." I blushed as the crowd applauded and could hardly wait to get off the stage.

On a warm spring Saturday afternoon in Bayside, when I was thirteen, Cookie, Gene, and I climbed into our old blue Plymouth with our foster dad. We were heading to one of my favorite activities—our dance lessons at the Foundling. Winding our way through noisy streets in the weekend traffic with horns blowing and cabs passing by, we finally found a parking spot just one block away from the Foundling.

Dressed in shorts and sports shirts, we piled out of the car and marched down the street with our black leather tap shoes in hand. Smiling as if we were on our way to stardom, we hoped to catch a glimpse of the firefighters training outside the tall red brick building directly across the street from the Foundling. And, we weren't disappointed.

It was fascinating to watch men climbing high ladders, then disappearing through a window, which could have been in burning building. I breathed a sigh of relief when they would reappear hanging on to a rope as they descended the building to the street below. I thought, *What brave men to choose such a dangerous job.* We didn't want to leave, but knew Mr. Henry was waiting for us. We arrived just in time. Students between the ages of eight and fifteen gathered on the long wooden floor visiting with one another as we slipped into our tap shoes. Mr. Henry's commanding voice brought us to attention.

"Line up in two rows over here—boys in back and girls in front."

Standing like a cadet along with the other students, our veteran instructor picked out three of us girls. Noting the perfect curvature of our legs and the way our calves touched, he commented, "Pretty legs—you'll look attractive on stage." His words burned in my ears as I imagined that *maybe someday I would be a Rockette!* (I later learned that the height requirements for the internationally known troupe are the same today as they were during Radio City's opening night on December 27, 1932- between five foot six and five foot seven. I had to give up on my dream to join those long-legged beauties; I only grew to five foot four. However, I proudly carried Mr. Henry's compliment with me for many years.)

After taking lessons for two years, I was selected to be a member of the Foundling's dance troupe—three boys and three girls who performed for civic clubs and community gatherings. On one occasion, wearing our maroon and gray uniforms while dancing on roller skates, we appeared on

TV. Performing with the Art Henry Dance Troupe was a real confidence booster for me. Meeting new people and traveling to civic clubs and community events was expanding my horizons.

Christmas at the Foundling

An air of festivity electrified the Foundling's auditorium the afternoon of the annual Christmas party. Foster parents and youngsters entering the room, clamoring to reserve a front seat, found themselves gazing at the towering Christmas tree that stood next to the piano. It was laden with white twinkling lights and dozens of ornaments. The area in front of the stage was decorated with gifts in colorfully wrapped boxes, all donated by generous New York stores and collected by firefighters.

As I hurried backstage, my heart was pounding. Performers huddled in tiny dressing rooms putting on their fancy costumes just in time to line up before the curtain opened. Lights blinked and the noise hushed to a murmur as people scrambled for their seats.

Sister Baptista announced, "Welcome to our annual Christmas Variety show! You are in for a very special treat. Our children have a wonderful afternoon planned for your enjoyment—singing, dancing, and Christmas presents!" Children's eyes sparkled with anticipation as the lights were turned low and the red curtain slowly opened. Looking official, wearing maroon and gray uniforms, our troupe stepped forward in a single line towards the audience and danced to the upbeat tune, "There's No Business Like Show Business." The crowd loved it!

One child with blonde curly hair twirled on her toes in her shiny pink ballet costume to the enchanting "Music Box Dancer." At the finale, the audience joined the young performers singing "Silent Night" and "Joy to the World." For me, this was a snapshot of how exciting it must be to dance on the stage of Radio City Music Hall. This audience of displaced children, watching their peers entertaining the crowd, was having the time of their lives. Separating myself from the crowd and moving over to the piano bench, I began softly playing "Jingle Bells."

"Ready for presents everyone?" a nun asked.

"Yea!" the crowd yelled. She called the children up by age groups beginning with the youngest. Filled with delight, they lined up holding their foster parent's hand and waited their turn to sit on the jolly big-bellied Santa's lap. "Silver Bells," "Dashing Through the Snow," and other well-known Christmas carols rang out through the auditorium until all the gifts but one was given away. When the last person walked out of the hall, I climbed off the piano bench and quietly walked towards Santa to receive my gift.

"Thank you Janice, you made this a special afternoon for all of us," a nun said, smiling. It didn't matter to me that I was last; I was glad I could bless the audience with my music—the only gift I had to give.

Tragedy Hits Home

My foster mother, Lucy, had two sisters, Ginger and Tillie. Aunt Ginger was the youngest—always smiling and pretty with her curly blonde hair and red lipstick. She was the thoughtful, fun-loving, rabble-rouser of the bunch and lived forty-five minutes away in Brooklyn with her husband, Pete. Playing show tunes on the piano and entertaining us with her keen sense of humor made our visits to her apartment a lot of fun. Opening an envelope addressed with our name on it from Aunt Ginger on our birthday or Christmas was a rare treat. As foster children, we seldom received mail from anyone.

Her older sister, Aunt Tillie, was tall and slim with white hair. She was a kind, gentle nurse who lived for a while in the nurses' quarters, where she worked at Flushing Hospital in Queens. Never married, her warm-hearted compassion extended to the neighborhood stray cats, which would come running to her from all directions the moment she stepped outside her two-story residence. Because she was diagnosed with cancer when I was a teenager, Aunt Tillie moved to a hospital in Harrison, NY. She went through several grueling rounds of chemotherapy, eventually having a mastectomy. After her hospital stay, Lucy invited her to move into the cozy pink attic room on the third floor of our home to recuperate. We loved having her live with us. We didn't hear her complain once about anything, not even climbing the two flights of stairs up to her room.

The stress of having a house full of kids and a sick sister in our home sometimes caused my foster mother's anger to get out of control. One day while she was trying to diaper one of the babies who squirmed, as babies often do, she whacked the little one's bottom a few times. This brought a quick response from Aunt Tillie.

"Lucy," she'd plead. "She's just a baby—don't hurt her!"

"Leave me alone," Lucy responded. "I'll take care of these kids my way."

Frustrated, she would sadly shake her head and go back to her room.

One morning, when I was thirteen, I had to go to the Foundling for a dental appointment. As my foster mother and I returned to Bayside, and within a block of our home, we saw red lights flashing from emergency vehicles. Driving closer, we noticed police cars, a fire engine, and an ambulance—right in front of our house! Curious neighbors lined up as men in uniform were taking command of the area. Jumping out of the car and briskly walking up to one of the policemen, my foster mother frantically asked, "What happened?"

He hesitated and answered slowly, carefully, "A lady hung herself." Seeing the shock on my foster mother's face, he gently touched her arm.

"Tillie...oh my gosh, Tillie..." Her voice trailed off as she ran up the front steps into the house. We didn't realize that Aunt Tillie was already in the ambulance. Standing a few feet away from the police officer, my knees became weak; the flashing red and blue lights and faces of the people blurred as I almost fainted.

My nine-year-old brother, Gene, had found our precious Aunt Tillie in the basement, dead, hanging from a rope tied to a rafter in the ceiling. She had committed suicide. Not knowing what else to do, he ran across the street to the rectory. Father Ryan called 911, then came into the house and cut her down.

My heart ached as I solemnly watched the white ambulance with block red lettering drive down the street and out of sight. *I'm never going to see her again.* Then a wave of guilt, remorse, and sadness washed all over me at the same time. *What if I had not gone to that dental appointment? Would Aunt Tillie still be alive? And what about my poor brother Gene? How will he ever be able to survive this?*

Although Aunt Tillie never complained about her physical pain, the hopelessness and despair must have been unbearable for her to take her life.

"I Want You To Be My Baby"

In 1954, when I was fourteen, an eighteen-month-old baby named Ingrid was placed in our home. Despite the extra care needed for this dear child with Down syndrome and clubfeet, my foster parents made room for her.

I made a love connection with this little angel right from the start. Her outstretched arms reaching to hug me from her playpen when I returned home from high school was the highlight of my day. I picked her up, embraced her, and began singing "I Want You To Be My Baby," one of the top ten songs at that time. She would yell out repeating my words as I sang,

THE Good THE Bad AND THE Ugly

"I...
I want...
I want you...
I want you to...
I want you to be...
I want you to be my baby."

Ingrid and Jan 1954

As I sang the last word of the song, she threw back her head and laughed hilariously, as only a small child could do. Putting her back in the playpen, while watching her cheerful eyes, I sat down and began playing the piano as she bounced up and down to the music. One of the sweetest joys I ever knew was Ingrid's delightful laughter.

After living with us for one year, during her annual physical at the Foundling, the doctor found a mole on her right hand.

"It needs to be removed," he somberly told my foster mother. Ingrid was admitted to the hospital immediately.

Returning home from school the next day, I was distraught when I went into the living room where she often greeted me. Walking slowly to the piano, I mechanically placed my hands on the keys. Oh, how I missed her voice and sweet smile. And worse, I wondered, *What would the lab reports indicate?*

Sitting together at the breakfast table in the kitchen the morning of Ingrid's surgery, the telephone rang. As my foster mother answered, I immediately had a strange feeling in the pit of my stomach. Longing to hear that she was okay, my heart had an unexplainable sinking feeling. My foster mother softly mumbled, "I see...thank you." Hanging up the phone, she sadly looked at us and simply said, "Ingrid died." Slowly turning away and shielding her eyes from us, she walked out of the room. Stunned by the news, Peggy sat motionless; Gene ran into the backyard; and I raced up the stairs to my bedroom and stuffed my face into the pillow. We each grieved in our own private way.

55

It was uncanny; I knew in my heart that Ingrid had died before my foster mother told us.

Distressed that my two-year-old darling was now gone, and finding out that complications during surgery caused her to smother from the anesthesia, made me furious. When I heard there would be no funeral for Ingrid because her relatives were unknown, I was more outraged. I could not believe it.

"That's not fair! She deserves a proper burial." My face turned red as tears flowed. After my foster mother talked to the nuns about my feelings, the Foundling agreed that giving Ingrid a proper burial was the right thing to do.

Dazed, I stood sobbing before the tiny white casket in the dimly lit funeral parlor, wishing my precious sweetheart would wake up. Believing that she is with Jesus, running around with perfect feet, gives me comfort. I look forward to the day when we will meet again; filling heaven with our voices as we sing "I want you to be my baby…"

A Hardened Heart

Just before graduation from the eighth grade in 1954, Pastor Sharkey had a surprise for me.

"I see something special in you Janice, and would like to sponsor you to attend a private Catholic high school." Feeling honored that he believed in me, I was asked to discuss it with my foster parents. But like a drenching rain on a holiday parade, my foster mother's response was, "She's not going to any other school except the public school where her brother and sister are attending." Disappointed in her decision and the fact that my foster father let her controlling manner overtake any thoughts he might have had on the matter, I went to a public school, trying hard not to be resentful.

In spite of my foster mother's unpredictable personality, I was constantly looking for ways to please her. On her anniversary, birthday, or a holiday, I gave her cards, cakes, presents, and a corsage. But as she got older, and more foster children came to live with us, sometimes six to eight at a time, the pressure seemed overwhelming. Knowing she would open her home to just one more child put a lot of stress on all of us. The never-ending chores of grocery shopping, cooking meals, and constantly cleaning the house added to the strain and crowded her days.

Early one morning, I awoke to loud voices coming from downstairs. I heard my foster mother yelling at my older brother and sister. In anger, she threw a bucket of water on the kitchen floor for them to clean up because they had not cleaned the house before school exactly the way she wanted it. She treated them awfully. Her outrageous outbursts of anger scared me. My escape was pulling the covers over my head and asking God to let me die.

One evening at dinnertime, Lucy caught Peggy, fourteen at the time, feeding her spinach under the table to Bunny, our Cocker Spaniel.

She shouted, "Get away from the table and get down into the cellar! Don't you dare come up until I say so!" The cellar was a cold, dark place that housed old furniture and heavy clothing set out for drying on the clothesline. Nervously looking back at us with a pitiful gaze, Peggy opened the door and slowly descended the staircase, step by step, into the darkness.

Suddenly, we heard a piercing scream as she fell to the bottom of the stairs. Fear gripped my heart as I sprang from the table and frantically ran down to Peggy's motionless body lying on the cement floor. Sitting down and tenderly cradling her head in my lap, I whispered, "Peggy…Peggy…please don't die!" Sobbing, I looked for any signs of life as I adjusted to the darkness. She finally opened her frightened eyes and looked up at me. I patted her head and whispered, "Everything is going to be all right, Peg. It will be all right." My foster mother suddenly appeared at the top of the stairs.

"You get up here right now, or you'll stay down there with her!"

I hugged Peg one more time and then, regretfully, left her and nervously climbed the staircase to the kitchen. Avoiding eye contact with my foster mother, I ran upstairs to my bedroom and cried for an hour. Peggy survived the fall, but my emotional recovery took much longer than my sister's physical healing.

Returning home from school when I was fifteen, I heard screaming coming from the upstairs bathroom. Racing up the stairs, I saw my foster mother kneeling at the bathtub clutching Gracie's head as she was washing her hair under the faucet. The three-year-old toddler was petrified of water. Her eyes were filled with terror as she cried, "No, no, stop!" Trying to restrain her, my foster mother accidentally pricked Gracie's soft skin with her nails; she began to bleed.

"Stop hurting her!" I shrieked. "She's just a baby. I'll wash her hair!" My voice trembled.

"Get out of here or I'll throw you out of the house!" Lucy glared at me and determinedly went back to scrubbing Gracie's sopping brown hair. I sheepishly backed away and retreated into my room. A little while later my bedroom door opened and Gracie ran into my arms with a towel wrapped around her body. Her arm was bleeding, and she quivered all over with tears in her eyes as I put ointment on her wounds. Assuring her everything was going to be all right, I carried my little princess to her bedroom, tucked her in, and kissed her goodnight.

When she turned twelve, her birth mother took her back home to live with her. But by the time she was a teenager, her stepfather raped her night after night. Gracie believed that her mother knew about it. The abuse was never reported.

Foster children sometimes endure cruelty and ridicule, and many times they are treated badly in their own homes more than anyplace else. After being abused by her stepfather, she married an abusive man who battered her for years. The cycle of abuse continued; she ran away from him into the arms of another abuser.

Years later, I visited New York and cringed to see Gracie so anxious that she could barely finish our walk around the block where she lived. Riding in a car, taking an escalator in a department store, or even riding in an elevator was difficult for her. Medical problems were a constant companion, and it broke my heart to see my sweet girl grow up bound by these phobias.

My foster sister did eventually marry a nice man. Unfortunately, it ended in divorce after a few years. But she did have one special blessing—her beautiful daughter, Jennifer, who was the love of her life. Grace died suddenly from a heart attack in July, 2010. She had forgiven everyone who hurt her and is now a peace with her Heavenly Father forever. She was fifty-five years old.

One day, while Lucy went grocery shopping, I decided to surprise her and clean the entire downstairs of our house. I could hardly wait to see her delighted expression when she returned home. Instead, walking in the door and looking around the house, in her controlling manner she said, "I didn't tell you to clean the house. Why did you do it?" I was disappointed and angry with myself for expecting to get a compliment.

In spite of her outburst, I tried not to get discouraged and still tried to please her. (I think the term for that sickness is called co-dependency.) Before leaving for her women's auxiliary meeting at the Foundling, I helped style her hair and put on a light shade of lipstick. She had beautiful skin, and it didn't take much effort to make her look nice. A smile and a hug as she walked out the door were all I needed to carry me through the day; however, the feeling did not last for long.

"You'll never amount to anything!" she would shout as her face reddened when we did something that displeased her. "You're the scum of the earth! Look who your parents were!" Threatening to send us back to the Foundling if we didn't shape up left us frightened, emotionally fragile, and insecure. She was tearing away our dignity.

I loved my foster dad, but didn't like the fact that he was a pushover and rarely stood up for us kids. Many times when he returned from work, she greeted him with the bad news of the day and ordered him to discipline us. Instead of giving us the hug we longed for, he'd swat us on the rear; I think it hurt him more than it hurt us.

At fifteen, Joe mouthed off at Lucy as we sat around the breakfast table. With fury in her eyes, she picked up a coffeepot and threw it across the table at him. He ducked! It missed him and landed on the floor as the rest of us jumped, sitting wide-eyed and speechless.

Joe became bitter over his turbulent years in foster care. As an adult, many years later he sent me this note hoping I would get in touch with reality:

A wide-opened hand slap in the face was not uncommon. The abuse was not only physical, but verbal as well. One of her favorite statements was "You lousy Lowery's!" Our emotional well being was being destroyed and any sense of self-esteem was non-existent. She was a breeder of inferiority and we couldn't do anything about it. I tried to run away several times, but I'd be sweet-talked by Lucy smoothing out my misery. She didn't want anyone to know what was really going on behind those walls. Inner conflict was a steady companion.

Despite Joe's inner struggles, and perhaps because of them, he took on the role of the family clown. His sense of humor helped lighten up our fragile emotions caused by our foster mother's volatile temper. This delightful gift to make us laugh was appreciated by all the children in the Brennan's home. In a letter written to me years later, Cookie recalled:

Joe, the clown, jokingly impersonated Barbara, who had Cerebral Palsy. He would mimic her running out the front door of our home to catch the yellow bus that picked her up to take her to a school for disabled children. He put on her hat, coat and scarf, and while we were sitting around the dinner table, he spastically walked through the front door with her cane and threw the whole family into hysterical laughter. Barbara, who had a wonderful personality, laughed most of all.

As the Lowery children grew older, Aunt Grace, our birth mom's sister, called one day to tell Lucy that our mother was begging for us to visit her in the hospital at Rockland State Institution. Lucy's response to us was, "Your mother is no good. Your parents are drunkards and not fit to be around." We were silent and didn't dare answer back. Perhaps our foster mother never forgave her for the rejection we received on our first visit when I was ten. She added, menacingly, "If you visit your mother, you'll get kicked out of here and be sent back to the Foundling Home. You'll end up in a place much worse than here. And, if you say anything to the social worker when she visits, you'll pay the consequences when she leaves." Believing her vicious threats, we didn't say a word to anyone about how we were being treated. And as teenagers, we never visited our mother again.

While I was sixteen, I rebelled and didn't want to practice piano anymore. My performances began to decline, so I quit taking music lessons. My foster mother was furious! Her dreams for me—for us—went up in smoke. Demanding that I pay back every penny she spent on my lessons, her attitude towards me became cold and callous. As a senior in high school, I worked part-time at the soda fountain in the Horn & Hardart Automat in Flushing, Queens to pay her back. It was good to get out of the house, and I was glad that there would be no more practicing, no more performing, and no more music—for now.

Like baby birds snuggling in a nest, each child who came into our home found a special place in my heart. We knew they would not be ours forever, and even though they would eventually transition to a family that really wanted them, it was hard to let them go.

More often than we cared about, that moment of departure would arrive. As our family stood waiting in the living room, a car would pull into the driveway and strangers would ring our doorbell. The social worker had come to remove one of our little ones, two-year-old Kenneth, so he could begin a new life with new parents. Grabbing my camera to take a last photo of him wearing his snuggly blue coat and hat, my foster mother and I kissed him and placed him into the social worker's arms. Getting into the car, they threw kisses at our family. We stood on the curb waving until the vehicle drove down our block, around the corner, and out of sight forever.

In the beginning, I believe my foster mother's motives for bringing children into her home were honorable. But Joe said, "She's just doing it for the money." Never believing that, Joe labeled me as *the dreamer*—and not in touch with reality.

THE Good THE Bad AND THE Ugly

Free at Last

High school graduation is a milestone that students normally celebrate with enthusiasm for the future. If nothing else, it marks that period of time when teens are not required to go to school and are free to cut loose and move on to the next phase of their lives. Chances are, relatives one may not have seen for years will show up to cheer you on. Such was not the case for me. In fact, I vaguely remember that day in June of 1958.

Using my Brownie Hawkeye camera, I think Cookie might have taken the picture of me dressed in my cap and gown. Memory escapes me why none of my foster family saw me graduate. There was no party, no fanfare, and no family acknowledgement of this milestone in my life.

Graduation Day 1958

Senior Prom was the social event of the year. Tony, my tall, slim, Italian boyfriend who had graduated in 1957, arrived at our front door looking handsome wearing his white tuxedo coat, bow tie and black pants. Wearing a beautiful pink calf-length strapless gown with crinoline petticoats, I descended the staircase in the hallway of our home and walked into the living room. Tony smiled and presented me with a white carnation wrist corsage. Then he whisked me off to the dance at Bayside High School in his sleek red 1958 Chevy. I felt like the belle of the ball. We danced and danced and then drove into Manhattan. Ordering drinks and food at the enchanting Hawaii Kai restaurant in the posh Lexington Hotel helped me forget about being without family on this special day. Tony treated me like a princess as we watched a landscape scene of Hawaii on the wall of the restaurant change from a brilliant yellow sunrise to a golden orange sunset.

Riding the Staten Island Ferry, marveling at the rainbow of colors reflecting the New York skyline on the water was spectacular. As we passed the illuminated Statue of Liberty, Tony linked his arm through mine, kissed me, and said how much he appreciated our evening together. He was a guy I could always depend on. We were falling in love, but after leaving a strict foster home, I was not ready to get married. I wanted to spread my wings, travel, and experience life. We remained friends for years and eventually went our separate ways.

A month after graduation, I celebrated my eighteenth birthday. Now my liberation was complete! Just as I was free from the public school system, I was also free from the foster care system with all its rules, regulations, and requirements. But in those days, it also meant being cut off from all dental and medical benefits and other safety nets.

My foster mother laid down the law when the Foundling cut me loose. "Earn a living and get a job." So, instead of going to college, or moving away, I rented the small attic room where Aunt Tillie had lived and remained there until I was twenty years old. Lucy still wanted to enforce curfews on me. I made an effort to oblige—but not for long.

Moving out of the house where I lived since I was seven was a big event. Now on my own, I moved into an apartment upstairs in a private home with a backyard in Fresh Meadows in Queens, New York. I had now become an independent woman! Even though it was small (my living room was also my bedroom off the small kitchen and bathroom), it was a far cry from the large home in Bayside where I grew up. Wanting to show off my new place, I invited my foster mom to see the apartment. She liked it! But, to my surprise, because the apartment was so small, she decided to sell the piano that I practiced on throughout my childhood. She had promised it to me. Apparently that did not matter. She got rid of it and did not say a word to me. My heart sank when I found out she sold that beautiful Baldwin Baby Grand to a piano teacher for $25.00.

Foster Parents of the Year

Sister Catherine, Sister Baptista, Cookie, Peggy & Jean, Jan, Barbara, Gene, Monsignor Daniel McGuire, Charles & Lucy Brennan, Grace and Louis

In 1959, the administrator of the Foundling Home announced that our foster parents had been chosen as "Foster Parents of the Year." We were all surprised when our foster mother told us the news and asked us to join Dad and her at the Foundling for the presentation. With mixed emotions, Cookie, Peggy and her two year old daughter, Jean, along with Barbara, Gene, Gracie, Louis and I attended the celebration.

On one hand, I was happy to see them being acknowledged. They had made sacrifices to give us a good home. And on the other hand, I was bewildered that they received this honor, despite the turmoil that plagued our young lives for years.

Not knowing why people act the way they do, I had to look for their good points and not focus on the bad stuff. I am grateful that our physical needs were met—delicious food on the table, clean clothes, a bed to sleep in, and a roof over our heads.

At times I wondered, *Since they've kept us for so many years, why don't they adopt us?* I later found out we were not eligible for adoption because we had living relatives. We never knew the reason our aunts or uncles could not or would not visit us or come to our aid.

Larry Mercer, former Director of Buckner Children and Family Services in Dallas, heard my story, shook his head and said, "Jan, the worst nightmare of the foster care system is to place a child in what they thought was a loving home, yet be unaware of the destructive behavior of the foster parents behind the scenes." Children pay a high price when agencies with staff who are overloaded and underpaid, are unable to read the emotions of children who are too afraid to say anything about their circumstances.

But, to look at the positive side, The New York Foundling Home today has a reputation for helping thousands of children over the years. They celebrated their 140th anniversary in October 2009, with a Mass at St. Patrick's Cathedral followed by visits to the Foundling located on 17th Street and the Avenue of the Americas in New York City.

I have discovered that the good, the bad, and the ugly moments in my life were stepping stones to the ministry adventures I am experiencing today. God's plans for me were unfolding when I didn't even realize that He had His hand on my shoulder every step of the way.

Chapter Three

Small Steps to Great Adventures

Corporate America

In today's world most parents encourage their children to get a good education and make a successful life for themselves. Back in my high school days, my foster mother told me that I needed to get a job and earn some money. Consequently, I followed in the footsteps of a friend and got a position in Manhattan with the Metropolitan Life Insurance Company. Traveling an hour and a half each way to type policy cards in an all-girl office turned out to be the most boring job in the world. After six months of this drudgery, I resigned.

New York City Skyline

However, Manhattan fascinated me. Each street had its own personality—Fifth Avenue with its exclusive shops, Park Avenue's expensive apartments, and Broadway's gigantic lights, ethnic

67

restaurants and nightclubs. On Fridays, my favorite date night, I took in a Broadway play and enjoyed dinner at one of New York's unique restaurants in the theatre district. Frank Sinatra called New York the city that never sleeps, and he was right. I took advantage of every opportunity to experience its diversity.

After quitting my job at the insurance company, I accepted a position as a secretary with Bank of America International in the downtown area on Wall Street. When the bank moved across from the New York Stock Exchange on Broad Street, I became a secretary to one of the vice presidents on the international floor. Learning to communicate with corporate executives and interacting with people from overseas dressed in their native costumes was opening up a whole new world for me. Visiting the Stock Exchange on my lunch hour or taking a trip on the Staten Island Ferry while cruising past the Statue of Liberty, gave me a deep appreciation for the strategic landmarks in the city where I was born.

Since my foster dad worked only a few blocks from me, meeting him for lunch was a nice diversion in the middle of the day. Walking through the historical Trinity Park churchyard and cemetery was an outing that made us wonder about the people who came before us. I recently discovered that Trinity Church is home to New York's social elite of the past; Alfred Tennyson Dickens, the son of Charles Dickens, is one. He came to New York to coordinate the centennial of his father's birth. On the eve of the celebration, Dickens suffered a fatal heart attack at the Hotel Astor and died. Because Dickens did not have next of kin in America, he was buried at the cemetery with a gravestone donated from Trinity Parish.

Just a stone's throw from the Twin Towers in Manhattan, Trinity Parish, founded in 1697, became better known after the terrorist attack of 9/11. On September 19, eight days after the terrible attack that rocked the nation, the church reopened its doors for workers who spent hours ... days ... months ... digging in the rubble where the towers once stood. It became a refuge, a place for quiet reflection. On the doors of the church, the welcome sign read: *Enter...Rest...and Pray.*

One of the perks of working for Bank of America was the opportunity of participating in the weekend activities made available to employees. This was a new experience for me. Because foster children often get transferred from one home to another, many times they don't get to be part of a team. In our home, we weren't allowed to join in any activities; we had to come straight home from school. So, as a young adult, when I learned about the weekend ski trips, I was first in line to sign up.

Heading for the slopes on a chartered bus with co-workers to Mount Snow, Vermont, was quite an experience for this first-time skier. Once we arrived, lining up at the incredible buffet and stuffing ourselves late at night, wasn't a healthy thing to do. But we enjoyed every bite. And staying up till the wee hours of the morning socializing with old and new friends didn't make it easy to hit the slopes at the crack of dawn. But we did it anyway. Snow plowing out of control towards the outdoor heated swimming pool made me realize that skiing didn't come naturally. My leg muscles paid quite a price for this strenuous activity. Even though I didn't lead the pack in the ski department, I enjoyed the fresh mountain air and drinking hot toddies at the end of the day with friends. I had a great time. But, sleeping on the bus all the way back to New York and barely making it to work on time the next day, didn't allow me to be my best on Monday.

After working three years at the bank, I wanted a more challenging and financially rewarding job. In 1962, I resigned and went to work for the Thoroughbred Racing Association (TRA), the FBI of the racetracks.

Pushing through the revolving door to the lobby of the eleven-story Daily News Building, an enormous globe—the largest

She Dares to *Dream*

in the world—greeted me each morning. Huge clocks with time zones of countries around the world hung from the walls surrounding the globe. My gaze lingered on the timepiece with the hour of France on it, dreaming one day I'd travel there.

Stepping off the elevator on the ninth floor, I walked past United Airlines to TRA at the end of the hallway. My well-paid job entailed handling insurance claims for officials of the *Sport of Kings*, as they called racing in those days. Learning the rules of racing and meeting owners of the top horses in the country, including the Triple Crown winners and their jockeys, was fascinating. Not knowing much about gambling, I managed to bet two dollars on a favorite to show and came home a winner every time, much to the amazement of my associates. Sitting in a box seat reserved for celebrities in Belmont or Aqueduct racetracks with owners of the greatest horses in the nation made me feel like a queen.

Jan at Thoroughbred Racing Association

The TRA office was located in the mid-town section of Manhattan. The United Nations Building, with its colorful international flags flying on top, and the famous Grand Central Station were remarkable sights close to where I worked. Walking along the East River with the wind blowing my hair and watching tugboats pulling ships many times their size along the riverbank, made me feel like I was watching a documentary film showing the amazing diversity of New York. I could hardly tear myself away from the dancing waters, and many times got back to the office on the brink of being late.

One day while everyone in the office was out to lunch, I heard these sharp words crackle over the radio: "John F. Kennedy has been shot in Dallas!" I couldn't believe my ears. When my bosses returned to the office, I told them the unbelievable news. Stunned, one co-worker remarked, "How could this happen to our president?" That evening, while walking to the subway on my way home, a silence I had never experienced in New York filled the air. People passing by had tears streaming down their faces, and even cab drivers weren't blowing their horns. The city was in total shock. Little did I know that someday I would be living in Dallas not more than thirty minutes from that tragic site.

Globe Trotting Adventures

As a young woman, I yearned to travel and see the world, and that opportunity soon came my way. I was in the right place at the right time when I discovered TRA, United Airlines, and IBM all located on the ninth floor of the Daily News Building. Sharing the same restroom and listening to the stories of women with beautiful tans traveling to exotic far-away places piqued my interest. Even though I was making a good salary for a twenty-one—year old who had never been to college, I was intrigued and wanted to travel and do something more challenging.

In 1963, a year and a half after working with TRA, I interviewed at United Airlines and took a test for part-time employment. The questions were so difficult, I wondered if I was being tested to become a pilot. A week later, an employee of United dashed into my office at TRA and said, "Jan, you're hired! You can start next week." I was thrilled, but kept my daytime job at TRA. I worked in the evening as a reservation agent from 5:30 to 9:30 p.m. It didn't take long for the mad pace to drive me crazy. I had lots of money but no time to enjoy it.

One night while out with a group of friends, I met a man from IBM at a dance in the Taft Hotel in Manhattan. A girlfriend introduced me to this tall, handsome man with salt-and-pepper hair resembling the famous talk show host, Johnny Carson. His good looks and ability to dance were important qualities to me at the time. We were crazy about each other and dated almost two years before he proposed. Our wedding date was booked; the flowers were ordered; and the invitations were ready to go out. But, I was troubled, and a feeling I couldn't explain prevented me from mailing them. The expression *no peace, no permission* ruled the day. Not having peace about the wedding, and after realizing that he was not *the one*, it was called off. I was relieved but also physically and emotionally drained.

Finally resigning from TRA and keeping my twenty hours a week with United, I became a secretary for an executive vice president. By joining the credit union, I saved enough money to buy a green 1965 Mustang convertible, which I still own today. Building some lifelong friendships, along with the travel privileges, made me a very happy employee.

Jan – United Airlines 1965

To supplement my income, I took temporary jobs as an administrative secretary for a Kelley Girl agency. Getting to choose the days and hours I wanted to work was perfect for my lifestyle. Enjoying assignments at television stations, advertising agencies, modeling studios, and working with retired executives wasn't the least bit boring.

Sitting at a front row table at the Copa Cabana or dining at a fine restaurant and meeting famous people became familiar to me. One evening after work, a friend took me to Jilly's, a spot that Frank Sinatra frequented, where I was introduced to a charming, handsome man named Charlton Heston, the famous movie star featured in the movie, *Ben Hur*. Another evening, while strolling with friends along Third Avenue in Manhattan, we entered a small cabaret and were greeted by two famous movie stars, Sammy Davis, Jr. and Peter Lawford. Being invited to their table and exchanging *star* stories, then singing popular songs, resulted in a very enjoyable evening.

Working in the city, traveling to faraway places and having the funds to splurge, was an exciting life to live. My brothers became envious reading my postcards from exotic places and decided to go to work for an airline themselves. Joe got a position at British Overseas Airways (BOAC), and a few years later Pan American hired Gene. We three Lowery foster kids stretched out of the box and entered into the fast world of travel.

In her early twenties my foster sister Cookie met John, a Turkish doctor of internal medicine, at a party in Queens where we lived. She fell in love and went to visit him in his country for a vacation. We were expecting her back home, but she stayed in Turkey and married John. In 1964, I took my first overseas trip to Balikesir, where Cookie had given birth to her first son, Rizar. Since neither of my foster parents had been on an airplane, I invited them to join me on the trip. Declining my offer because she was afraid of flying, Mom told me, "You'll never get Daddy on an airplane." Much to her surprise, at the age of fifty-five, he took the plunge and joined me on his first airline trip from New York to Amsterdam to Istanbul. When I clued in the attendants that this was Dad's first flight, they treated him like royalty. I could tell by his sweet smile that he was really enjoying himself.

Landing in Balikesir and stepping out of our small Turkish plane, was like walking into a different world a hundred years ago where people either traveled by donkey or walked. It was obvious that our cultures were very different. Trying to buy stamps at the post office with men breaking in line in front of me was my first signal. Cookie's husband, John, eventually stepped up to the counter and made the purchase.

SHE DARES TO *Dream*

Cookie's ability to learn the language, the customs, how to cook Turkish foods, and how to fit into another world was really impressive. The kind hospitality of her husband's family and the Turkish people was wonderful.

On our return trip, Dad and I stopped in Rome, The Eternal City, where we toured St. Peter's Basilica. Seeing the Pope addressing hundreds of people from a second-story window of the Vatican in St. Peter's Square on Sunday morning was meaningful. Growing up in the Catholic Church attending the Latin Mass, allowed me to understand the ceremony. After the Pope's sermon, Dad and I toured Rome in a horse–drawn carriage with an Italian coachman who didn't speak English. We laughed together as I directed him to the sites we wanted to visit, by pointing to pictures of the locations in my tour book. We managed to see some of the most important sites in Rome—the Ruins of the Forum, the Coliseum, and Trevi Fountain where Dad deposited his Turkish coins. Making history with Dad on his first and only international trip was fantastic.

Foster dad and Jan in Rome, Italy 1964

Back then, airlines offered their employees *fam* trips—up to a ninety percent travel discount on a first-come, first-serve basis. Signing up every opportunity I could, traveling became a priority on my agenda.

On one of these fam trips, I flew with a group of airline employees to Paris, France. Leisurely walking past the incredible *Arc de Triomphe* and watching artists selling their colorful paintings along the Seine River was exciting for this young woman who dreamed years ago of moments like these. I mustered up the courage to taste escargot (snails) for the first time at a bustling sidewalk café at three in the morning. I actually liked them! Enjoying a walk along the Champs Elysees early in the day, and gazing up at the remarkable Eiffel Tower in the evening, made me feel like I wanted to stay forever.

Flying back home, entering the doors of the *Daily News Building* and looking up at the clock on the wall showing *Paris* time brought back fond memories of a beautiful city.

In 1966, my brother Joe was supposed to get married, but a week before the wedding, it was called off. Since we both enjoyed traveling and he had already purchased the tickets, he asked me to join him on what was supposed to be his honeymoon. We traveled to Spain and Germany. Joe was determined to have a good time in spite of his broken heart.

On one memorable occasion in Madrid, Spain, we walked into a small café that was showing a bullfight on the TV. It was terrifying watching a huge animal charging the matador, who was swinging his red cape and missing him by inches. With my eyes half closed, I watched a few more passes as the crowd stood to their feet pointing thumbs down and roaring, "Kill! Kill!" It sent chills down my spine. This disgusted me and was not my kind of entertainment. We stood up, paid our bill, and walked out.

The next evening we enjoyed fabulous flamenco dancers and a great dinner. This was more like it!

A few days later, we took a train to Munich, Germany, where the aroma of sausages and sauerkraut filled the air as we walked past street stands in the evenings. Touring the beer halls and watching the stout waitresses wearing their colorful costumes winding through the tables with large steins of beer dangling from their fingers on both hands was quite a sight. Families ate, drank and belted out German drinking songs with gusto. An attractive, blonde-haired German girl captured Joe's attention, and from then on, I was on my own. I didn't see him again until we boarded our plane back to the states.

In the meantime, I decided to do some touring on my own. Squeezed together with tourists in a cable car climbing 10,000 feet to the top of the Zugspitz, the highest mountain in Germany, I witnessed a visual feast for the eyes. The view of the snow-capped city below was breathtaking. Carefully stepping off the tram, I walked to a huge lounge with dark-paneled walls and a crackling fireplace, where people dressed in stylish ski outfits sat on deep couches sipping their favorite hot chocolate or martini. Looking out of the floor-to-ceiling windows, I saw people walking on a narrow path leading to a large gold cross overlooking an enormous cavern. I didn't have the courage to step out there.

When I spotted the baby grand piano in the corner, I felt compelled to ask the manager, "May I play a few tunes?"

"Certainly!" he replied. "Everyone would love it." As I walked toward the piano I thought, *This mountain paradise is about to be turned into a concert hall.* As I ran my fingers up and down the keys, the crowd quieted down immediately. The notes rang out as clear as a bell on the extraordinary grand piano. A standing ovation followed as I hit the last note of "Malaguena." I thought, *Maybe all that practicing as a child was worth it.*

Music, the international language, always bridges the gap between people of different ethnic backgrounds. And, not being able to speak the German language didn't prevent me from being invited by a group of guests that day to attend a party in the beautiful city of Oberammergau. This is the home of the famous Passion Play that takes place once every ten years.

The time had arrived to take the tram back down to the village. As my new friends and I made our slow descent, I marveled at God's awesome creation. The view of the town below with church steeples peeking out of the snow and lights twinkling in the distance was like a picture postcard.

A few days later, I discovered Garmish, a beautiful, quaint town that borders Germany and Austria where I met an American girl at a lunch counter. She was living in the country to learn the language. The young woman worked at a guesthouse where I ended up renting a room and staying for a week. Enjoying a delicious bratwurst sandwich with sauerkraut, potato salad and an ice-cold beer was the best! Ice skating in this village with my new friend translating for me was extraordinary. She opened the door for me to experience the people, the culture, and the food first hand. The week was over much too soon.

On my last day in Germany, I strolled by myself past shops, restaurants, and the train station, wondering, *Since my mother was of German decent, did any of my ancestors walk these streets or ride these trains too?* Perhaps one day I'll have the answer ...

Chapter Four

Dream On

As a young woman, I dreamed…. *of my husband and me, sitting in cushioned white wicker rocking chairs on the porch of our lovely one-story home, overlooking a large body of water. Sounds of laughter fill the air as we cuddle our grandchildren on our laps. Pink geraniums and white daisies decorate the flower boxes on the verandah, as curtains blow past the homemade pies cooling on the windowsill. Pets are barking, lively music is playing, and our family and friends are having a grand time together.*

Eleanor Roosevelt, a former first lady, once said, "The future belongs only to those who believe in the beauty of their dreams." So, I *dream on.*

My Prince Charming

On a beautiful day in May 1966, I drove my green 1965 Mustang convertible to Martels, a charming sidewalk café near 86th street in Manhattan. As I pulled up to the curb, my friend, Hillary, motioned for me to take a seat on the patio where we sipped tea as we chatted about our dreams and our future. Her enchanting English accent kept me hanging on every word. Excusing myself from our table to make a phone call to my sister, Peggy, I opened the door of the café and walked past a tall handsome blonde man sitting at the end of the bar reading a race car magazine. Attracted to him, I told my sister, "There's a good-looking man sitting at the bar who looks like the TV star Dr. Kildare. I'd sure like to meet him."

Peg replied, "Let me know if you do." Hanging up the phone and walking past this stranger to the outside patio, our eyes locked, and I knew we had made a connection. It seemed like I was drawn to him like a magnet. Returning to the table, I told Hillary what happened. Suddenly, the café door opened and the mysterious man walked toward us, appearing as though he was about to pass by. But to my surprise, he slowed down and winked at me. I thought, *If I don't say hello now, I might never see him again.* As he drew closer, I looked up at his smiling face and asked, "Do you wink at every girl you see?"

He responded, "Oh no, they have to be at least as pretty as you." Without giving it a second thought, I invited him to join us. He pulled up a chair and we introduced ourselves and sipped ice tea together. After a short conversation about his job at the Prospect Park YMCA in Brooklyn and tidbits of information about our lives, he said, "I have a friend returning from Mexico late this afternoon. Would you ladies like to join us for dinner?" Without hesitation, I responded, "Yes, that sounds wonderful."

It turned out that Hillary had other plans and Bill's friend, Pete, wasn't available to join us. So, to my delight, it was just the two of us. Phoning United Airlines and telling them I wouldn't be able to work that evening was a call that would change the course of my life. It wasn't commonplace for me to be undependable or to go out with someone I had just met, but good or bad, I agreed to go to dinner with this stranger.

"Where would you like to go?" he politely asked.

I suggested one of my favorite spots—the Oak Beach Inn on Jones Beach. "It's not fancy, but it is a fabulous seafood restaurant."

"Sounds good to me...let's go!" he responded. Opening the door on the driver's side of the convertible for me, and then hopping in on the other side, we headed for the ocean. With my dark brown hair blowing in the wind and my new handsome friend beside me, I felt free and happy without a care in the world. Over dinner, he fascinated me with stories of his college days in Mexico and adventures as a picador—one who irritates the bull in a bullfight and attempts to weaken him by pricking his shoulder muscles with a lance. Wanting to change the conversation, since I didn't like bullfights, I asked him to tell me more about himself. He continued to capture my attention with stories of his days as a paratrooper in the U.S. Army. I thought, *This is obviously a brave man of courage or a man who is totally insane.* I was enamored, and his warm personality appealed to me. After our delicious fish dinner, we took a short walk, enjoying the cool ocean breeze as the sun set on the ocean. We had our first kiss and in my heart, I knew I had met my *Prince Charming.* Eight months later we were married.

On our wedding day, my heart was filled with joy as the large black shiny limousine pulled in front of Sacred Heart Catholic Church in Bayside. It was right across the street from where I grew up. Wearing my long white satin gown and bridal train decorated with French lace, I carefully stepped out feeling like a Princess who was about to marry the man of her dreams!

Soft music played as guests were escorted to their seats. Friends, co-workers, and my foster family and siblings waited for the magic moment to arrive. Father Schmidt, wearing his black outfit covered by a white tunic, walked out from a side door to the front of the altar with Bill and his best man, Pete, at his side. The organ music signaled, and the guests stood to their feet; the back door of the church opened slowly and the small procession began.

My nine-year-old godchild, Jeanie, looked like a little doll, carrying a small basket of white carnations, as she walked down the aisle in her long gold satin dress; Jeannette, the beautiful maid of honor, followed in her full-length green satin dress. Looking refined in his black tuxedo with gray striped pants, my foster father took my arm as the majestic Lohengrin's "Wedding March" rang throughout the sanctuary. With stars in my eyes, I proudly walked down the aisle with my dear foster daddy, gazing into the eyes of my beloved *Prince Charming*. I felt confident as I drew closer to the man I was about to marry and live happily ever after. The only sadness I felt was that my sweet new husband had no family members present.

*Standing Left to Right-Grace, Jeanie, Jan and Bill, Gene, Louis
Seated-Peggy, Joe, Lucy and Charlie Brennan*

My total savings of $900 was invested for a reception at the charming Blue Spruce Inn on Long Island. When I selected the location, it was mid-afternoon and the sun shined radiantly through the stained glass windows, reflecting rainbows across the room. I knew this was the place for our once-in-a-lifetime reception. Our seventy guests enjoyed a delicious buffet dinner.

When it was time for our first dance as a married couple, Bill and I danced to the dreamy "Hawaiian Wedding Song." Later, my foster father and I danced to "Daddy's Little Girl." A formal wedding, a wonderful reception, and a honeymoon in Hawaii! *What could be more romantic!* I was a young bride stepping into a whole new world with expectations of love, romance, and a life filled with happiness.

Flying first class to the islands on a United Airlines jet was an exciting way to start our honeymoon. We began our lives together on the enchanting island of Oahu, where delicate leis were placed around our necks as we entered the airport. One of the first performances we wanted to see was the famous Kodak show on the beach. We watched beautiful, long haired Hawaiian girls dancing in their flowing grass skirts to the island music of the famous Don Ho. To top off our afternoon, we drank milk out of a freshly cut coconut as we walked along the beach watching the churning deep blue ocean waves. I felt like I was in paradise.

Visiting the Pearl Harbor exhibit the following day was our next stop. What a shocking remembrance of the tragedy when the Japanese attacked Pearl Harbor on December 7, 1941. Touring the island and experiencing the beauty of the flowers, the warm, clear water, and the friendly people, was wonderful. In spite of all this beauty, I couldn't quite understand why Bill seemed a bit guarded and sometimes distant during our honeymoon. He said that everything was all right, but I nervously wondered, *Did I make the right decision? Does he really love me?*

Returning home, my prince surprised me as he gallantly carried me across the threshold and up the stairs of what was now *our* tiny apartment. Everything appeared great, but what happened next totally shocked me. The first words out of his mouth were to let me know who was going to wear the pants in the family. He tried to make light of it, but I was upset.

Putting that incident behind me, I wanted to be the best wife that I could be. To me that meant having his eggs, bacon and biscuits on the table, making sure his shirts were spotless, his house was cleaned, and dinner was on the table when he came home from work. He never missed getting a kiss before he left for work and again when he returned home. The bottom line was, I really loved my husband and wanted to have a strong loving marriage.

A Family to Grow On

In 1967, I met Bill's precious mother, Ada, in Bessemer, Alabama. Her simple wood-frame house, where she lived for years, was her castle. Regardless of my New York roots, this southern lady and I connected as soon as we met. She was a sweet, tall, slim woman who welcomed me with open arms. When I entered her living room, I was drawn to a small picture in a plastic frame on a table in the corner. I walked over and picked it up. Staring at it, I could see that it was Jesus standing and knocking at a door without a doorknob. Back then I didn't fully comprehend the meaning of this picture. But now, I realize that the door had to be opened from the inside. I have learned that Jesus is a gentleman who stands at the door of our hearts waiting for us to invite Him in. Little did I know that this image would become one of my most prized possessions. After all these years, I still have it displayed in my home office in Dallas, Texas.

By the end of July that same year, our precious daughter, Lisa, was born. Bill drove me in the Mustang convertible to Doctor's Hospital in Manhattan. Recognizing the urgency of the moment, a nurse whisked me into a wheelchair and took me immediately up to labor and delivery. By the time Bill parked the car and returned to the hospital, our baby girl had been born.

A few days later, we brought our daughter home to our tiny upstairs apartment in the two-story home where I had lived before our marriage. The L-shaped kitchen, one bathroom, and a living room that overlooked our fenced backyard became our humble dwelling place. We slept on a pull-out sofa and ate our meals at a folding card table. Lisa's crib fit perfectly in a small nook at the end of the kitchen. Our small quarters in Flushing, Queens, didn't bother me because we had a roof over our heads, food to eat, and a family that I loved with all my heart.

A year and a half later, the phone rang and it was Bill's former boss from the YMCA in Brooklyn, New York.

"The Multiple Sclerosis Society needs some help here. I'd like you to consider coming to Dallas." Bill discussed the move, and said it would be a good opportunity to get out of New York. But, I had mixed emotions about moving. The idea of leaving my family and friends didn't excite me at all. Our family dinners, Sunday picnics in the park, and holiday celebrations were important to me. I didn't know anyone in Dallas, but when the man I loved wanted me to move, I agreed. We didn't have many possessions, so it didn't take long to pack up, say good-by to family and friends, and start our new life in Texas.

In 1968, Bill flew ahead to Dallas to get situated with his new job. A month later, my eighteen-month-old princess and I flew to Big D. Pressing her nose against the window and looking at the puffy white clouds, I watched her and wondered, *What in the world will life be like in Texas?* My anxiety eased when Bill's charming new secretary, June, greeted us at the airport and invited us to lunch for Mexican food at El Fenix. That evening, Bill met us at the hotel where we stayed until we found a place to live. It was a wonderful reunion, and our Dallas life had begun.

Moving to a new state without knowing a soul and Bill traveling Monday through Friday was not to my liking. A few weeks later, we found a two-bedroom apartment close to Bachman Lake near Love Field Airport. During the daytime, I packed a picnic lunch and took Lisa across the street to play at the park at Bachman Lake. We fed the ducks and took long walks along the water's edge. In the evenings, my little girl and I sat on the back steps of our apartment overlooking the runway, waving to the pilots as they crossed the lake before landing at Love Field.

"Is that Daddy's plane?" she'd ask as they flew over Northwest Highway. She would make a sad face when I explained that

Daddy would not be home for another week. We could hardly wait for Fridays to arrive.

Sitting at the airport in our convertible, watching plane after plane land, seemed like forever. Then, the magic moment would arrive.

"There's Daddy!" Lisa yelled as she stood on the seat of the car waving. We greeted him with smiles and kisses and headed home to our nearby apartment.

After living in Dallas for six months, I suggested to Bill that we search for a small house of our own instead of paying rent each month.

"Jan, you are never satisfied," was his response. Wanting more than my parents had and building a nest egg was important to me. Finally, Bill agreed. With the help of a realtor, we found a three-bedroom house on Lynn Street in Richardson. It had a one-car garage and a fenced backyard. Bill enjoyed working in the garden planting tomatoes and string beans; my enjoyment came from planting a pretty flower bed with Lisa by my side.

A few months later, we were thrilled to announce that I was pregnant with James. My heart was filled with love as I nursed our new gift from heaven, born August 7, 1969. We were shocked when the doctor told us that James had jaundice and would have to stay in the hospital until his blood count was balanced. As I held him in my arms each day, I wondered, *Is this the day I can take my baby boy home?* More than a week had passed before we finally made our grand exit from St. Paul's Hospital in Dallas.

The moment we arrived home with our new bundle of joy, Lisa ran to the front door and greeted her baby brother with a kiss on his forehead. Now, our family was complete. I loved being a stay-at-home Mom. There were moments I would not have wanted to miss for the world. With Bill traveling each week, our backyard garden became my sanctuary. Sitting on the swing set singing songs with Lisa and James were precious moments. Watching our dachshund, Schotzie, chasing Peter Rabbit around the backyard made for an afternoon of hilarious laughter.

However, motherhood wasn't always the way I thought it would be. One of my most interesting adventures was going to the laundromat when Bill was out of town. Juggling one infant on my hip, with a toddler around my leg and pushing a large basket of laundry with a box of detergent from home was tricky. Searching for quarters to put into the machine and then entertaining my little ones as the clothes were being washed was another challenging experience. Once the clothes were washed, switching them to the dryer was almost impossible. By the time I got home, it was naptime—especially for me.

Bill & Jan, Lisa & James

Wanting to create a beautiful home without the financial resources wasn't easy. Other than necessities, I could only dream about the items I would like to make our home more attractive. As a little girl, I often stood in front of the china cabinet in our living room watching the rainbow of colors bounce off the shiny cut crystal bowls. When the sunlight hit them in the afternoon, it was mesmerizing.

Learning that my foster parents were leaving Queens, New York, and moving to St. Petersburg, Florida, I thought, *This might be a good time to ask mom if she would be willing to let me have a piece of the beautiful crystal that I admired as a child.*

With apprehension, I dialed her number to make my plea.

She answered, "No, we're giving most of it to the Salvation Army. It would get broken transporting it to Florida or sending it to Texas."

Her tone of voice told me there would be no negotiating. My heart dropped, and I thought, *How could she be so mean? She knows my birth family didn't have any treasures to pass on to me.*

Apparently, a love for crystal was innate in me since an early age. I'm grateful that my home in Dallas is filled today with gorgeous crystal pieces that dear friends have given me as precious gifts over the years.

Making it Work

Wanting to keep our marriage strong, I tried to put my best foot forward and learn about activities Bill enjoyed. He introduced me to a whole new world of camping, fishing and boating. And I loved it! We decided to camp our way down to Ft. Lauderdale to visit his brother and family.

Disregarding the previous conversation I had with my foster mother, I still wanted my children to have a relationship with their foster grandparents. Since we would be passing by where they lived in Florida, I decided to call and see if we could stop by and visit. After making my request, there was a long pause.

"That's not such a good idea," she finally said. "I'm not feeling well these days and I'd rather not have any company." Again, I allowed myself to feel hurt, rejected, and was sorry that I called. What I realize today, is that we cannot change people. The only thing we can change is our attitude toward them.

Nevertheless, in the summer of 1972, being young and a little bit crazy, we pressed ahead and armed ourselves with sunglasses, sunscreen, swimsuits, camera and water bottles. After packing our camping gear, playpen, and clothing, we finally loaded our ten-month-old nursing baby, James, and three-year-old toddler, Lisa, in our Mustang and headed to Ft. Lauderdale. Setting up our tent, cots, food, and playpen nearly every other night was a bit strenuous. This was not luxury living. And once we had everything in place, it seemed like it was time to pack it up again.

Relieved, we finally arrived at the home of Bill's brother. His family was fun to be with and our boating experiences were a sight to see. I ignored the men's snickering as I baited my hook with gloves on to catch my first fish. Driving the long way home we decided that someday we might take another vacation—but something a little less hectic.

Not having much of a budget for baby sitters and entertainment, we made Friday our big date night at home. After putting our little darlings to bed, we enjoyed my cooking expertise as we sat at our romantic dining table with candles, a nice meal, and a bottle of wine. We listened, and sometimes danced, to the soothing music of Trio Los Panchos and Frank Sinatra. "Strangers in the Night" reminded us of that beautiful sunny day we met at the sidewalk café in New York. Everything seemed wonderful and since we were dining at home and not driving, we felt like we had a license to drink; nothing was wrong with that…or so we thought.

I longed to go dancing with Bill, but he wasn't interested. However, with the encouragement of some friends to join the "Cadence Dance Club," he agreed to take the plunge. Dressing up in our best duds and heading from our small home in Richardson to a fancy country club in Dallas made me feel like a grown up Cinderella. Looking dignified in his dark blue suit and tie, with me dressed in my long chiffon evening gown, Bill escorted me into the elegant ballroom. We had a wonderful evening "tripping the light fantastic" to the jitterbug, the waltz, the cha-cha, and the mambo. Translated, Bill and I "danced the night away" as we enjoyed a sensational evening.

To bring in some extra money, I stepped into the world of sales and became an Avon Lady, with my three-year-old Lisa by my side. Keeping her out of my display case was tricky, but she loved being Mom's assistant. Mrs. Walker, our neighbor, looked after James as he napped and I worked for a few hours. A few years later, my next sales position was with a studio convincing mothers to sign up for a plan that scheduled a photographer to take portraits of their newborns at three months, six months, and again at one year. Mapsco was my closest companion as I diligently drove through the streets of Richardson finding the homes of new babies.

The *extra money* I saved added up. After working part-time jobs for several years, I went into a piano store and picked out a Yamaha baby grand. I paid cash for it and had it delivered the same day.

Being active at St. Paul's Catholic Church, teaching Catechism to grammar school children, as well as serving as publicity chairwoman and photographer for the Women's Guild kept me busy. Practicing the organ for the Sunday service with Lisa at my side was a challenge, but it was time well spent. One of the priests asked me to help coordinate the first Christmas pageant for the students in the school, with music, costumes, and decorations. I enjoyed the opportunity to be creative.

Playing the organ at the back of the church at St. Paul's on Christmas Eve, as I stretched my head to get a glimpse of my two children marching down the center aisle to the Manger, was difficult. Lisa, portraying Mary and James dressed as one of the three Wise Men, made me feel proud. Kodak made a lot of money that evening as parents flashed their cameras capturing memories of the Christmas story, which became an annual event at St Paul's.

Since I was a small child, I was taught that on Saturday you go to Confession, and on Sunday you go to church. There was no discussion about whether or not you *felt* like going. We were taught that it was the right thing to do. I wanted my children to learn these principals at an early age. To this day, I have kept the cards they wrote as children saying *Jesus loves me*. Lisa and James both received their First Holy Communion and the Sacrament of Confirmation as part of the Catholic tradition. Reciting grace before meals and opening the Bible on Good Friday was part of our Holy Week devotions. Studying the pictures of the Stations of the Cross on Good Friday interested my little ones.

It wasn't until my children turned sixteen that I encountered some resistance to attending church on Sundays. Bill was active in the men's club, but as the years went by, church was put by the wayside.

Sitting alone during services, watching families take Communion together and going out to eat afterwards, made me feel sad. How I longed for family togetherness, especially concerning church related activities.

In the 70s, after we moved to Richardson, Texas, a friend, Marie Danna, introduced me to the ladies of the Richardson Chorale Club, now known as the Contemporary Chorale. Becoming a member of the group and learning classical and popular music, became an important part of my life. Entertaining at churches, nursing homes, as well as public and civic events, kept this exciting Club active throughout the year.

Jan performing with the Contemporary Chorale

Growing up loving dancing made it a natural for me to suggest incorporating movements to the songs. "The Trolley Song" was my first venture, which resulted in my becoming the Chorale's first choreographer. I held that volunteer position for the next seven years.

Waking up in the middle of the night, my mind flooded with dance movements, I would head to the kitchen to jot down my ideas. Bill would get up and catch me dancing in the kitchen.

"What are you doing up at this hour?"

"I might forget the steps if I don't write them down!" I blurted. He shook his head and headed back to bed as I continued searching my mind for creative ways to make the songs more entertaining.

Admiring my black and white Ascot scene costume from "My Fair Lady," Lisa remarked after one show, "Mom you look pretty." She loved my long skirt and huge black wide-brimmed hat and gloves. It was like watching Mommy playing "dress-up." Her sweet words put the finishing touch on the evening.

In 1976, the Bicentennial year, the Chorale gave eighty-two performances and received awards from the Dallas American Revolution Bicentennial Corporation and the Daughters of the American Revolution Bicentennial Corporation. The applause at our performances made all my late-night hours and extra rehearsals worthwhile.

A Crumbling Castle

Attending pancake breakfasts, bazaars, and St. Patrick's Day and New Year's Eve dances at St. Paul's Church filled our social calendar. As shocking as it might sound, during that era, it was normal to have alcohol available at church gatherings while the youth cleaned off the tables after the events. There was a lot of partying but little spiritual enrichment. Bill continued going to the men's club meetings, but eventually stopped going to church altogether.

In 1973, he lost his position with the Multiple Sclerosis Society. Being a hard worker, he searched daily for another job to provide for our family. He found a position and worked with a swimming pool company for several years. Later, a man in our church invited Bill for an interview with an electronics company. He got the job; but one evening at a party, one of the wives made a strange comment to me: "I hope your marriage survives this industry." I asked her what she meant by that statement.

She said, "A lot of partying goes on."

I assured her that in spite of some difficult times, we loved each other and were working on having a good marriage. But a few months later, there were social occasions where the wives were not invited. Alcohol destroyed my birth family, and I was terrified that it was destroying our marriage. Grumbling, sarcasm, disrespect, blame, and unforgiveness, all lead to division in a relationship. Our family has a history of alcoholism, and unless habits are changed, relationships crumble.

One day in 1982, without notice, Bill packed his bags and drove off. He moved into our first home in Richardson that we had rented out; it was vacant at the time. James was thirteen and Lisa was fifteen. After a two-year separation, Bill asked me to meet him at a restaurant. He spoke the last words I would ever want to hear—"I want a divorce." He didn't want to be married to me any more, and I, the dreamer, had to face reality. Being separated from my husband was not the worst thing in the world for me, but the word *divorce* never entered my vocabulary. On Valentine's Day, 1982, Lisa opened the front door of our home to a police officer holding divorce papers. There was nothing I could do. The children and I were shattered. After seventeen years of marriage, we were divorced in 1984.

The break-up was hard on all of us. But because I didn't want to dishonor their father, I did not discuss our issues with the children or my friends. Consequently, everyone was surprised at this *happy couple* going their separate ways.

Hanging out the dirty laundry of our marriage is not what I choose to write about. I have learned that once the dirty laundry is out—a clear view towards happy tomorrows is blocked and memories of blame and discord continue. I've learned to ask for grace through the tough times and to forgive when there is dissension. Most of all, I have learned to pray about everything. Without leaning on God, I wouldn't be able to release offenses.

It has taken me years to realize that finding a quiet place for intimate prayer helps me be still. My heart relaxes in His arms, and I don't have to prove anything. I choose to forgive and not seek revenge. Life is fragile and full of the unexpected. I know now, that through prayer and devotion to my Heavenly Father, I can get through anything as long as I have Jesus by my side.

On my first night out as a single woman, I attended a function with some co-workers from the newspaper where I worked. Feeling extremely uncomfortable and with tears streaming down my face, I found myself turning my back to the people who were gathered. I was not handling my new role as a single woman well and asked my friends to take me home.

As time went by, the publisher of the newspaper took me under her wing and taught me how to sell advertising. She was a great teacher and eventually promoted me to sales manager. Pounding the pavement doing business with spas, restaurants, clubs, and art galleries was exciting. However I would have traded it all for a good marriage. Unaware of Biblical principles and the promises of God, we didn't have a solid foundation.

♥ *"I am the vine and you are the branches.*
He who abides in me and I in him, bears much fruit;
for without Me you can do nothing"
(John 15:5).

Chapter Five

Destiny Plays a Part

The Touch of a Mother's Hand

On that terrible day when I first met my mother on the grounds of Rockland State Psychiatric Center, I was a frightened ten-year-old little girl. Her impersonal words, "I don't care who that G_d d_mn kid is! Get me a cigarette!" She had wounded my heart and I didn't want to see her ever again. But one day in 1973, my sister, Peggy, telephoned me in Dallas with some news. "Mom is really doing well. When I first saw her, she was living in a dormitory with thirty women behind locked doors and was being treated for depression and schizophrenia."

Feeling like a bolt of lightning had hit me, my mind was filled with questions. *When did she start visiting her? Why didn't she tell me?* She did not explain much, but because Peggy's husband was a compulsive gambler and left her for another woman, she had a need to be needed. Her visits to our mother were a real blessing because our Mom really needed her.

I did not know what schizophrenia was. Few lay people did. Researchers have not identified the causes, but they believe genetic factors play a role as well as chemical or subtle structural abnormalities in the brain. According to the Mayo

Clinic, some of the symptoms can be: hearing voices, fear that one is under constant surveillance, delusions, social withdrawal, difficulty in taking care of oneself, remembering simple tasks and depression. There is also a high rate of attempted suicide in people suffering from schizophrenia. However, with the right consistent medication, those suffering from the disorder can often function normally.

I never found out which of these symptoms our mother exhibited, but Peggy's visits over that year lifted Mom's spirits immensely. Because of her progress, the staff moved her from the bleak, overcrowded dormitory to a semi-private room in another building with her own dresser and closet. Escorted by staff, she attended church, ate lunch off the grounds, and even traveled to New York City to see a Broadway show. Her life had changed dramatically.

Peggy's contact gave me the courage to put aside my anxieties and meet this woman with an open mind that I hadn't seen since childhood. I agreed to fly to New York and drive upstate to see her, along with my sister and her friend, Jimmy. It was a beautiful brisk autumn day. Red, orange and yellow leaves waved in the breeze as we drove through the entrance of the institution. My anxiety was at its peak as we parked the car in front of a large red brick building.

"Let's go inside," Peggy said coaxing me to join her. I shifted nervously in my seat and told her that I would wait in the car with Jimmy.

As I mentioned earlier, in order to shield myself from future inquiries, I told people that my parents had died in a plane crash. Now that wall of protection I had built around my heart for decades was beginning to crumble. Like a Phoenix rising from the ashes, the mother whom I had buried in a tragic accident was about to resurrect from the dead and stand before me in living color. Peggy entered the building as I sat behind wondering, *Was I ready? Would I be able to face her after all these years?* Yes, I was finally ready to meet the woman I portrayed as deceased for all those years.

Glancing toward the door of the building, I saw Peggy emerge, smiling, holding the hand of a short stocky woman wearing a black coat flapping over her blue dress. Guiding our mom to the front seat of the car, Peggy slipped into the back with me. My mother immediately turned around, reached out her hand to me and said, "Hello, Janice... I'm so glad to see you." The warmth in her eyes, and the friendly tone of her voice relieved my anxiety. With my voice cracking, I took her hand and softly said, "I'm glad to see you also." My emotions were raging, and it was hard to hold back the tears.

My mother, Florence Lowery with my sister, Peggy Ferguson

Peggy announced, "Since Mom loves Chinese food, we're going to a great oriental restaurant off the grounds." Jimmy started the car, and we pulled away from the building.

Our mother was eager to catch up on a lifetime of missed moments. Taking a bite of chow mein, she listened as if the stories of her grandchildren were the most important words she would ever hear. I told her, "James is almost five with red hair and is a sweet little boy who loves hugs and smiles a lot." Her eyes were fixed on me.

"Lisa, your granddaughter, has beautiful blonde hair and is six years old. She's in the first grade and loves art and is taking ballet lessons." Peggy and Jimmy ate silently, giving me the floor. "My husband, Bill, works for the Multiple Sclerosis Society and travels a lot. He is a good father, and the children really love their daddy."

Mom then eagerly opened up about the recent events in her life. She told us how she loved going to Broadway musicals—perhaps some of the same shows I enjoyed as a child when my father took us to New York City. How ironic, I thought, *Even though I never saw Mom and Dad together, they both loved musicals just as their children did.*

In between mouthfuls of food, she said shyly, "I work in a factory, but I don't make much money. Could you send me some every now and then?" Initially, her question took me by surprise. On second thought, I realized she had no one else to help meet her needs. A candy bar, a newspaper, and a magazine all cost money. Her humble life, evidenced by the lack of visitors and small surroundings at the institution, left her with little opportunity to acquire any personal treasures. And, feeling more like a daughter with each growing moment, my heart melted. More than anything, I wanted to give her something that would be more meaningful than money. *What gift can I give this woman who has received absolutely nothing from her family?* Suddenly the idea came to put together a family album of my favorite photos for her. Mom's eyes brightened as she nodded with a big smile when I told her what I planned to do.

After paying the bill and leaving the restaurant, we got back into the car and drove back to the building where Mom's sparse room waited for her. Looking sadly at her two daughters, she stepped out of the car and pleaded, "Please come back again soon; I love you." She reached out to Peggy, and the three of us embraced.

I wanted our time that day to be pleasant for our mother; however, as we drove away, I had so many questions spinning through my head. I wondered, *Did she love our father? Did she remember seeing me as a little girl?* Regardless of having unanswered questions, I was pleased that we had the opportunity to reconnect. The years of fear, pain and rejection that kept me from knowing my birth mother melted in that one endearing moment by the loving touch of my mother's hand.

Destiny Plays a Part

On another visit, Mom totally surprised Peggy and me when she sat down at the piano in the visitors' lounge and played a medley of Broadway tunes! Mom couldn't read music, yet entertained us as though she had years of lessons. Never did I dream that my mother had that kind of ability. Her eyes sparkled as Peggy and I applauded along with the nurses, patients and visiting relatives.

Music makes the heart happy, and she willingly gave us the only gift she had.

A year later, I took a trip to New York with my seven-year-old daughter, Lisa, so she could visit her grandmother for the first time. Tightly clinging to my hand while looking to me for assurance, we walked up the long staircase to the second floor of the three-story building. Slowly opening the door to the reception area, we saw mom waiting for us on the couch in her simple orange dress. Smiling, she jumped up and reached out with both arms towards Lisa.

"Hello darling!" Mom's voice bubbled and her eyes sparkled as she wrapped her arms around her granddaughter. Seeing her grandmother, a total stranger, for the first time was a little awkward for Lisa, but she smiled sweetly and hugged her back.

"Come see my room," Mom offered, extending her hand to her granddaughter. Watching Lisa walking down the hallway holding her grandmother's hand warmed my heart. Cuddled on the bed together, slowly turning pages of the family album I had sent, Lisa described the pictures with great detail. Relieved that the visit started out so well, I watched Mom drinking in the information as though it were an oasis in a parched desert. I thought, as I shook my head, *So many lost years. So many memories that were not a part of her life.*

Mom could hardly wait for us to meet the staff and other patients on the floor. Leading us down the hallway, she stopped each person telling them "This is my daughter, Janice, and my granddaughter, Lisa!"

When it was time to leave, she didn't want us to go. "Please come and visit me again," she begged as we hugged and promised to return some day.

Feeling guilty about my mother living in an institution, and me not doing anything about it, bothered me a lot. I had made all sorts of selfish excuses—my family life was going well, my children were doing fine, so why rock the boat? *But is this what a loving daughter would do? Just ignore the situation?*

One evening when the children were in bed and Bill was traveling, I had a glass of wine and nervously picked up the phone and dialed the institution.

"I'd like to talk to Florence Lowery," I told the receptionist. My heart was pounding as I waited for a voice at the other end.

"Hello, this is Florence."

After a quick introduction, I blurted out crying, "I want to know if you'd like to come and live with me in Texas?" There was a long silence. Then she said some of the most significant words I had ever heard from my mother.

"Janice, you are where you belong, and I'm where I belong. Take good care of your family and that will make me very happy."

With a shaky voice I said, "I can't stand to see you spending any more years in that hospital!"

She responded, "Janice, I'm really content where I am… honestly." She sounded convincing, and somehow I was relieved. When I hung up the phone, the heavy burden of guilt I had felt for so many years had lifted. I could now go on with peace in my heart.

A Memory to Last a Lifetime

I can only imagine what dinners at the institution must have been like for Mom. *Five o'clock—get to the cafeteria. Line up and get your meal. What's new? Oh, not much. Wish I had more money so I could buy a magazine.* Day after day, week after week, the same routine.

The staff and patients must have become Mom's family, but I was sad that she never got to enjoy the day-to-day interactions with her children like I had with mine. She didn't get to watch the dance troupe perform or attend any of my concerts. Mom missed every birthday party and all the events that a mother would treasure, including my high school graduation.

But one day, our mutual friend, Wayne, a brilliant businessman who knew our story, generously offered his magnificent home in Connecticut so that Peggy and I could cook a meal with our mother. We didn't hesitate for a moment to say *yes*.

We picked up Mom one beautiful fall Saturday afternoon. Driving through rolling hills, past small white churches with tall steeples, to the swanky New England community of Darien, made me wish I lived there. Anticipation was high as we pulled up into Wayne's circular driveway, admiring the bright pink and white impatiens that bordered the shrubs in front of his home. I helped Mom as she got out of the car. She looked happy holding hands with both of her daughters as we walked towards the backyard.

Opening the back porch door, Wayne greeted us, dressed casually in a white sport shirt and khaki shorts. Extending her arms, Peggy hugged him and said, "Thanks so much for inviting us to your home." Beaming with delight, he led us to the blue deck chairs at the end of the rectangular-shaped swimming pool.

"How about some iced tea?" he asked.

"That would be great," I replied.

He went inside and Mom sat and listened as we lounged around the pool, telling more stories about her grandchildren.

Peggy commented, "Your granddaughter, Suzie, loves animals and wants to be a veterinarian; Jeanie, like most teenage girls, has her eyes on the boys."

After Wayne brought our iced tea in colorful plastic glasses, I joined the conversation giving the Dallas report. "I wish you could see Lisa wearing her pink ballet outfit on stage with her class dressed as tiny butterflies."

"I'd love to be there," she commented.

I added, "Watching James climbing the bleachers at the football games carrying a trombone larger than his body is quite a sight to see."

As the afternoon lingered on, I thought, *What a shame that she missed the most important moments in the lives of her children and grandchildren.*

This day was significant not only to our Mom, but also to Peggy and me. We could tell by her sweet smile that for the first time, she was thoroughly enjoying herself with us outside of the institution. The sun glistening on the water and the aroma from the fragrant flowers made the atmosphere absolutely wonderful. Mom sat looking like a dignified lady having high tea at the palace with everyone paying attention to her. Mother and daughters, sipping tea, relaxing, chatting—*What could be better than this?*

The brilliant orange sun sank behind the trees as the afternoon began to cool into the evening.

"Anyone hungry?" Wayne asked.

"Oh, yes" replied Peggy.

Since he was a bachelor, we didn't expect him to have anything prepared. So, Peggy and I searched the tall wooden kitchen cabinets for something creative to make for dinner. We found a package of spaghetti in the pantry and the makings for a salad in the fridge. Mom, who had probably not cooked her own dinner for decades, looked on approvingly, reveling in the opportunity to be in a kitchen with *her girls*. Standing near the hallway, Wayne, with a grin on his face, listened to our conversation and watched our childlike antics.

"It's all yours," he said, retreating to his chair in the den with a martini in hand.

With a little help from Peggy, Mom set the dining table and I put the water on to boil. Peggy handed her a jar of tomato sauce to heat, while I chopped lettuce and tomatoes and created my special vinegar, oil, and garlic dressing. Allowing us to have our first *private* dinner together, Wayne remained in the den reading his newspaper.

Soon, the aroma of the Italian spices from the bubbling spaghetti sauce filled the room. Our dinner was ready. With Mom sitting at the end of the formal dining table, we felt like dignitaries attending a banquet for the queen. Joining hands and bowing our heads, we said grace before the meal. Peggy served the salad, and then passed the bowl of spaghetti.

"Delicious tomato sauce, Mom!" We chuckled as we ate our meal smothered with our gourmet sauce out of a jar.

"I'll have to come to Dallas to cook spaghetti sauce for you again," she said.

After dinner, we cleaned the kitchen, joking and chatting about losing weight and telling our beauty secrets. Before we knew it, Mom's curfew time drew near. I wandered into the den to tell Wayne how much we appreciated his hospitality. Sitting in his brown wingback chair, he looked up from his paper and grinned, "It's my pleasure, Jan."

After drying the dishes, Peggy and Mom entered the living room, arm-in-arm, and also thanked Wayne for having us at his home. Looking shyly, he gave Mom a hug and walked her out to the car. I got into the back seat, while Mom climbed into the front next to Peggy. Her dancing eyes slowly saddened with the thought of returning to the institution. Peggy started the engine, shifted into gear, and pulled out of the driveway. Waving as we left, Wayne threw a kiss and went back into his house.

Little did we know that this would be our first and our last dinner party with our mother. It was a memory that would have to last a lifetime.

♥ *"Let not your heart be troubled, neither let it be afraid"*
(John 14:1).

Chapter Six

Letting Go

Hearing the Silence

October in New York is one of the most beautiful months of the year. Brilliant red and orange leaves fall to the ground like a graceful ballet of color. It wasn't my plan to visit upstate New York, but when Peggy called with the sad news that our biological mother had died, I flew there the following day.

Peggy and I arrived at the institution early the morning of her funeral. We comforted one another as we slowly walked to Our Lady of Peace chapel where our mother attended Mass on Sundays. A nun greeted us and took us to view her small casket sitting on wheels in the vestibule. Tears spilled from my eyes as I glanced at her wearing the white silk blouse and pink jacket she received from me some time ago. I wanted Mom happy and knew that she would feel proud attending the Broadway shows in New York wearing that classy outfit.

Being a musician, I couldn't help but notice that there was total silence in the chapel—no singing, no music, only silence. I thought, *She deserves more than this.* After getting permission from one of the nuns to play the organ, I ran up the creaky, wooden stairs to the dusty old relic of an organ that looked like it hadn't been used in decades. Since there was no sheet music available, I played some hymns from memory.

Looking down from the choir loft through my tears into a nearly empty church, I watched my mother's small brown casket being rolled down the center aisle with a large spray of red roses on top. Peggy took her seat in a pew next to the coffin. A handful of nuns and aides straggled in, took their seats, and the service began.

A Monsignor said the Mass, made a few comments, and then served Communion. Our mother lived on these grounds for forty-three years and this simple service was indicative of the simple life that she lived. Not many people were with her during her lifetime, and not many were present at her funeral. However, what I am most grateful for is how God orchestrated this moment in time, giving me the privilege of bringing my gift of music to her on this very significant day. Heaven is the finish line, the ultimate prize to all those who believe. She was devoted to her faith and she believed.

It is Finished

Now that both my birth parents had passed away, my father in 1954, at the age of forty-nine, and my mother in 1983, at seventy-one, I longed for my children to have a relationship with their foster grandparents. Never having a grandparent in my life, I often felt left out when people spoke about their treasured memories of their relatives. So, believing that people can change, I visited my foster parents, who had moved back to Queens. My children, Lisa and James, were two and four years old when we took the trip together. They seemed to bring out the best in their foster grandparents—dad's tenderness and my foster mom's rarely-seen, kind-hearted personality. Treasuring every moment, I wondered, *Why couldn't it have been like this when I was younger?*

A few years later, my foster mom had skin cancer on her leg. With a busy family of my own, and not much money for traveling, I didn't visit New York very often. But, during these difficult days, Cookie, my foster sister, traveled all the way from Turkey to Queens, New York, to comfort her. I flew in from Dallas but didn't arrive in time to say goodbye. She passed away just before Mother's Day in May 1987 at the age of eighty-eight. Our God is a merciful God, and I pray that she is in Heaven walking on golden streets passing a garden of Lilies of the Valley, her favorite flower.

During her funeral service I thought, *I did love her, and I will miss her. But I won't miss the rejection and always bending over backwards to please her.* When the service was over, the words that ran through my mind were those that Jesus said at His death, "...It is finished..." (John 19:30). Looking sad and helpless at the burial site, Dad whispered, "Jan, I did the best I could." With my arm around him trying to give him comfort, I said, "Daddy, that's all any of us can do."

It had been years since our foster family was together, so we took this opportunity to have a family gathering at my brother Gene's home in Bayshore, Long Island. Peggy, Gene, Cookie, Grace, Louis, and Joan, who lived with us a short time when she was little, gathered around to console one another, and let Dad know how much we loved him. My brother, Joe, disliked Lucy and he chose not to attend the funeral.

Breaking bread together and stuffing ourselves with a delicious buffet of sandwiches, pasta, cole slaw, and potato salad, was like old times. To top that off, we enjoyed an assortment of fabulous Italian pastries from Gene's favorite delicatessen. After eating the big meal, I commented to Dad that eating like this would make it hard to keep my girlish figure.

He responded, "Enjoy yourself sweetheart—you only live once."

A Celebration & A Bedside Melody

When Dad turned 90, I wanted him to have a great birthday celebration. So I flew to New York and surprised him at his fourth floor apartment in Elmhurst, Queens. Louis opened the door and was caught totally off guard. He said, "I don't believe it! Dad, guess who's here?"

With outstretched arms, I walked over to him sitting in his leather chair in the living room and gave him a kiss. "Happy Birthday, Daddy!" Smiling from ear to ear, he stood up and hugged me. After the surprise wore off, I told him, "There's a special birthday lunch planned, and I know you're gonna love it. So get dressed and let's go!" He got up and went into his bedroom.

As he walked back into the living room wearing a gray suit with a white shirt and striped tie, I said, "Pretty snazzy looking, Daddy." Escorting him into the elevator to the ground floor with Louis and Dad's aide, I could see the look of excitement in his eyes. As we stepped out the front door to the street, another surprise was waiting—a fabulous shiny, gray stretch limousine.

Dad was flabbergasted as he climbed into the vehicle.

"Nothing but the best for your ninetieth," I beamed. Dad looked like a dignitary riding into Manhattan with his private entourage heading for an important appointment. Reservations were waiting at the famous restaurant on Sixth Avenue—The Top of the Sixes—my *dream* setting for his special birthday. When we arrived at the tall building, a former boss and friend opened the door of the limousine and greeted each of us. He then escorted us to the fancy restaurant on top of the skyscraper. We were treated like royalty as he directed us to the best spot in the place—four seats at a window table!

Our waiter brought out a juicy filet mignon with potatoes and glazed carrots for Louis and Dad's aide, while I enjoyed a delicious grilled salmon salad. Despite the great assortment of main courses, a steaming bowl of mushroom soup and fresh bread with butter was all Dad could eat because of his sensitive stomach. As we took our last bite, he surprised me with a question.

"Darling, what are we doing here?"

"What do you mean?"

"This place is only for the rich people," he said.

"Daddy, we *are* the rich people. You are rich because you are healthy, and celebrating your ninetieth birthday! I'm rich because I have you in my life." He smiled, but I could tell he really didn't get it. Determined to make this day as spectacular as possible, I asked, "Daddy, would you like to take a carriage ride through Central Park after lunch?"

My Foster Father, Charlie Brennan and Me

He grinned and said, "I don't think so sweetheart; I'm a little tired." Relaxing in the limousine back to Dad's apartment, I could tell he was glad to be headed home. Living so far away in Dallas didn't allow me much opportunity to pamper him very often so I brought some flowers and cooked him dinner. Afterwards, I carried a small birthday cake with a few candles lit on top to the living room. With our happy voices, Louis and I sang "Happy Birthday."

Dad clapped his hands, and with a big smile said, "Wow, this is wonderful!" I reflected that, *This simple cake made more of an impression on him than my extravagant luncheon plans at the fabulous penthouse restaurant.*

Dad's comment about *this place only being for the rich people* was what he believed. And that's the way our foster parents raised us. However, I was grateful for the many good things they brought to my life ... and there were many. This day was my opportunity to say *thank you* in my own special way.

In Dallas, a few months later, the telephone rang, and when I picked it up, Louis' voice at the other end was trembling. "Dad's been in a coma for days, and it doesn't look good. He's in serious condition at Booth Memorial Hospital." I told him I'd fly to New York as soon as I could. Phoning the hospital staff, I said, "Please put a chair in my Dad's room; I'm catching a plane and would like to spend the night with him."

Looking out of the airplane window as we circled around LaGuardia airport, I cringed at the thought of seeing my foster dad in a state of helplessness. It was Christmastime, and as we were landing, it looked like a winter wonderland with the airport lights reflecting against the snow. Standing in line for a taxi with my luggage and portable keyboard under my arm, I turned my collar up to shield myself against the cold windy night air. It was finally my turn.

"Please take me to Booth Memorial Hospital as quickly as possible," I told the driver as I slid into the back seat. He surprised me and said, "I don't know where that is," brushing me off impatiently. Frost from my breath hung in the air as I hailed two more cabs—both refusing to take me to the hospital. Finally, I found a willing driver who revealed why they were reluctant to take me there. "It's such a short ride, and the fare is so little from the airport to the hospital that most drivers don't want to go."

Arriving at the hospital, I ran to the information booth and found out that Dad's room was on the fourth floor. With my heart pounding, I dashed into the elevator and then ran to the nurses' station, where they directed me to his room. Nervously approaching the bed, his eyes were shut; he was in a coma with tubes dangling from his nose and arms. Reaching for his limp hand, I took it into mine and whispered, "Daddy, I'm here, and will be with you all night." I wanted to stay in dad's room that night, but the staff failed to bring me the chair I had requested. To stay out of the way of the nurses, I ended up sleeping on the floor on top of my coat with a pillow underneath his bed. I was exhausted and fell asleep immediately.

Leaning over his bed and patting his head the next morning, I spoke to him as if he could hear every word. Placing my battery-operated keyboard on the side of his bed, I played some of his favorite tunes—"Put on Your Old Grey Bonnet," and "When Irish Eyes are Smiling." In the afternoon I played some Christmas carols as smiling nurses and patients crowded the doorway of his room.

The following day we received a phone call at Dad's apartment telling us the heartbreaking news—"Mr. Brennan is brain dead." Louis was devastated. Teary eyed, he said softly, "I can't let him go." He lived with Dad since he was a small child and had taken care of him for many years. It was now time to remove the respirator, but Louis couldn't give permission to do it. As God would have it, the following night, three days after I arrived, the doctor told us, "Mr. Brennan died peacefully in his sleep."

Four foster children—Joan, Louis, Gene, and I paid our respects to our foster daddy who had no biological children of his own, but loved and provided for so many. I sat near his coffin in the funeral home playing songs that he loved—"You are My Sunshine," "My Wild Irish Rose," and his all-time favorite, "Let Me Call You Sweetheart."

The service was held at St. Ignatius Loyola where my foster parents attended church for many years. We said our final goodbye at St. Charles Cemetery in Farmingdale, Long Island where Dad was buried next to Mom.

No Regrets

Letting go of relatives and those we hold dear is never easy. But to be able to say, "I have no regrets," at the end of a person's journey is a wonderful and peaceful feeling. To love and help people live well is the pathway to having that peace in our lives. Making fond memories today is what really matters.

To celebrate my sister Peggy's sixty-fifth birthday, on April 11, 2003, I flew to Florida. Our brother, Joe, drove in from California; but our youngest brother, Gene, wasn't feeling well and didn't make the trip. For the first time in ten years, the three of us were together, enjoying restaurants on the water, dancing on Friday nights, and just hanging out with one another. Enjoying a birthday cake and celebrating together was a rare treat.

During my early morning beach walk on my last day in Florida, I called my sister and asked, "Peggy, since today is Holy Thursday, could we have lunch together at your dining room table before I leave?"

She answered with enthusiasm, "Yes, that would be great."

I told her that after we finished lunch, I would like to have a Bible study at the condo across the parking lot where I was staying. "The whole family is invited to join us, but I won't be offended if some do not want to come." She understood.

Since Joe loves to cook, he prepared a delicious lunch. Knowing I would want to say grace before the meal, he said, "Hurry up, say grace and let's eat." We joined hands and I blessed the meal. After lunch I left and walked across the parking lot praying, "Lord, open the eyes of their understanding today and help them to grow spiritually."

About half an hour later, Joe, Peggy and her daughter, Susan, with her eight-year-old daughter, Gina, arrived at my door. With the aroma of a pine-scented candle filling the room, soft praise music playing, and a beautiful bouquet of carnations sitting on the table, they knew something special was about to take place. Conducting my first family Bible study with three generations present made my heart happy.

As youngsters, we attended church on Holy Thursday commemorating the Last Supper that Jesus ate with his disciples before He was crucified. Consequently, having this teaching outside of the church was new to my family. I explained, "Since Jesus blessed his disciples on Holy Thursday, I'd like to bless each of you today, and with your permission, serve Holy Communion."

I led them in a prayer asking God to forgive their sins. I knew that they were wondering, *What is she doing serving Communion?* As youngsters we were taught that only a priest or a pastor has the authority to serve Communion. I read the passage out of the Bible where Jesus said, *"...Do this in remembrance of me"* (Luke 22:19). He didn't say ... if you are a priest ... or if you are a pastor ... *then* you can serve communion.

We will have no regrets when we honor God by doing what Jesus told us to do. I served Communion that day, and as I said a blessing over each one, tears were shed and wounded hearts were being healed.

> ♥ *"To everything there is a season, a time for every purpose under heaven: A time to be born, and a time to die ..."*
> (Ecclesiastes 3:1, 2 NKJV).

CHAPTER SEVEN

A Search For Meaning

Digging Family Roots

After my biological Mom's funeral, I wanted to know all about her years in the Rockland State Hospital. The day she was buried, the staff at the institution presented Peggy and me with two binders containing Mom's entire history. On the first page was a photo of her the day she was readmitted to the facility in 1942. I cried as I saw her unhappy, hopeless expression and the resemblance of her features to mine. Sitting on a couch in the administrator's office, reading page after page of her transcripts, I discovered that recurring marital difficulties and alcohol abuse contributed greatly to their problems. This situation continued for years.

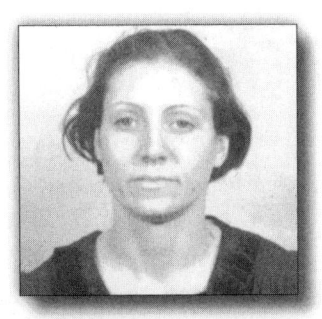

Mom was born March 9, 1912, in New York City. Armed only with an elementary school education, she worked as a salesgirl on Staten Island where she lived with her mother. She married my father in a civil ceremony on April 11, 1933, when she was twenty-one. Although I wanted to inhale both volumes that day, there was no time to read the entire story. I handed them back, and hoped to return soon and complete the task. But I never did.

Later that day, Peggy and I went to New York City to the Foundling Home, where we were placed in foster care as children. I tearfully explained to the nun, "Our Mom was buried today, and we came to find any information you might have about our family. We have a lot of questions. Where did our father and mother grow up? And why were we placed in foster care? We would also like to know why no relatives visited us?" After searching for some time, she finally dug up two old index cards with our biological dad's name on them.

"Your dad and his siblings grew up in a children's home in Mount Loretto, Staten Island—an institution for youngsters whose families were incapable of providing a good home for them."

Peggy and I looked at each other, shocked. After all these years, we had finally found some of our family roots. We learned that our biological dad was born February 7, 1905. Remarkably, February 7th was also our foster father's birthday. Still having a lot to learn about our heritage, I felt like I had only just begun.

Discovering where I had been baptized, I contacted the secretary at St. Brigid's Catholic Church in Greenwich Village, a few blocks from where my family lived when I was a baby. I told her about my life, and that some day I'd like to visit the church.

Compelled to find more answers, in 2003, I flew from Dallas to New York City to visit St. Brigid's Church. Gazing at the majestic, blush-colored church, while holding a fresh bouquet of assorted flowers I bought at a street stand, I wondered, *What secrets to my family's past does this old building hold?* I rang the doorbell and was greeted by a secretary who was expecting me. Handing her the flowers, she hugged me and said, "Janice! Please come in! I feel like I know you…"

"Thank you. I appreciate your willingness to help me find my parents records." Leading me down a narrow hallway into a small room with a large dusty bookcase, she reached for a leather-bound

A Search for Meaning

book from one of the shelves. It held handwritten records of marriages and baptisms that took place decades ago. Flipping through the worn pages, she stopped at one particular spot and handed it to me. As I scanned the names on the pages, I saw something I had not expected. My heart jumped as I discovered my Mom, Florence Lowery, though a Protestant, had converted to Catholicism. She was baptized in St. Brigid's Church on August 23, 1940, a month and a half after I was born.

I knew my parents were married in a civil ceremony, but I blinked with surprise as I looked at the pages before me. Mom and Dad evidently felt it was important for them to be remarried in the Catholic Church. The date of the wedding was August 27, just four days after her baptism. It was comforting to discover that Joe and Peggy were also baptized here, within a month of their birth. I also learned my youngest brother, Gene, was baptized in Guardian Angel Church in New York, a month after he was born. These records made me realize that as a young couple, religion must have been important to my parents, in spite of their problems with alcohol.

As I sat with the book open on my lap, I hungered to know more of my background. I wanted to go into the sanctuary where all these events took place and see the spot where my family stood over a half-century ago.

"I'm sorry," the secretary said, compassionately. "That area has been condemned. We're using the pews as a storage area right now. It's a mess."

"That wouldn't bother me at all," I told her.

She stood silently, reflectively, and said at last, "I think you are supposed to go in there." Opening the door to the

117

dark, dingy-looking sanctuary, manifesting its many years of obvious neglect because of lack of funds, I slowly entered and gazed at the altar.

"May I stand here alone for few minutes?" I asked.

She nodded, and left me there by myself. Walking slowly to the front of the church, sensing a holy presence, my head was spinning as I stood in this quiet place picturing the family celebrations that took place right on this spot. I thought, *If only these walls could talk. Who would have been at my parents' wedding? Did anyone take pictures at my baptism? Was the family all together here—the relatives we never knew?*

The answers didn't come, but what I discovered was that there *was* a Lowery family intact at one time, celebrating the precious moments and important events in their lives.

It was true, my parents started out in tough circumstances, not able to sustain the family because of the destructive forces of alcoholism and mental illness. But, as I stood at the same altar in the sanctuary where they were married, I realized they were good people, working through hard times. They longed for their children to grow up in the church and to have a better life than they did.

Children Without Dreams

I've often wondered, *How do you know that you are doing what God has called you to do?* My answer came when I visited a chapel in December 1988, on the grounds of Mount Loretto, where my father and his siblings grew up.

The sun was shining as I climbed up the subway stairs and walked to Battery Park at the end of Manhattan to board the Staten Island Ferry. Buying a warm cup of coffee and a bran muffin for twenty-five cents was my treat for the memorable ride past the Statue of Liberty. As the ferry churned into the docks across the sea from Manhattan, I searched for the bus that would take me to the orphanage. When it finally arrived, I stepped up and walked to the back of the bus. With white knuckles clutching my purse and heart beating with anticipation, I sat down for the forty-five minute ride to the other side of Staten Island. I wondered, *What secrets would I find in this place that holds so much of my family's history?*

"Mount Loretto!" the driver loudly called out. I quickly climbed down the steps to the street and began walking up the steep hill. All I could see was the peak of a building with a cross on top. As I got closer, there it was—the orphanage that I longed to see for so many years, with a two-story stone chapel standing alone in the distance. A smiling nun dressed in black greeted me.

"You must be Janice; we've been expecting you." Taking my arm, she guided me to the administration building where we visited in a small reception area.

"Your father and his siblings lived here during some very hard times. Many families had no money to feed or clothe their children, and were forced to give them up. Some of these less-fortunate children ran away to live under stairwells and on the streets of New York City." She gave me a pamphlet relating the history of Mount Loretto, and then left the room momentarily. I devoured every word.

> *Father Drumgool, a Catholic priest who was called the Shepherd of the Homeless Newsboys, recognized the need for a place where poor and abandoned children could live. In 1881, he purchased land at the corner of Jones and Lafayette Street in New York City, where he built the Mission of the Immaculate Virgin; a ten-story building that was the highest in the district.*
>
> *The following year, he decided to carry out his dreams—to build a vocational school to develop talent that would also serve as a home for the newsboys. He purchased a farm on Staten Island and founded Mount Loretto, which was the largest child-care*

institution in the United States. Children made their own clothes and shoes, grew their own food, and raised livestock and poultry. Soon Mount Loretto was able to care for 2,000 children and was debt free.

In 1882, Father Drumgolle organized the Mount Loretto brass band. They marched in every St. Patrick's Day Parade. It was one of the best in the country and they even performed at the White House.

I thought, *how ironic,* Dare to Dream Children's Foundation marched in the St. Patrick's parade in Dallas, and one of my fondest dreams was to conduct a class in the White House.

The nun returned to the room with a smile and asked, "Janice, would you like to visit the chapel where your father worshipped?"

"I'd love to!" I responded. Entering the chapel and sitting down to say a prayer, I thanked God for the opportunity to finally visit this significant building in my family's history. Imagining this chapel filled with hundreds of homeless youngsters, praying for a family of their own, brought tears to my eyes.

Chapel at Mount Loretto Orphanage

The original church was completed in 1894, and was magnificent. Sweeping her arm in the air, she explained, "The steeple rose 225 feet into the sky, and all of the pews, doors, and most of the trim were made by the boys in the Mission's grade school." She told me that the baptism scene in *The Godfather* was filmed here, and that many celebrities including Lou Gehrig, Babe Ruth, and Jack Dempsey visited the orphanage.

Walking upstairs she told me, "The original church burned to the ground, but the foundation remained and was used for the existing chapel." Slowly walking past the gallery of photos showcasing the orphanage since its inception, I viewed pictures of sad-looking newsboys in dirty clothes selling newspapers for food; others showed youngsters with hopeless-looking eyes staring into the distance.

One particular photo looked like a scene from a movie, showing hundreds of children standing in front of the orphanage with despondent faces, but nicely dressed and looking

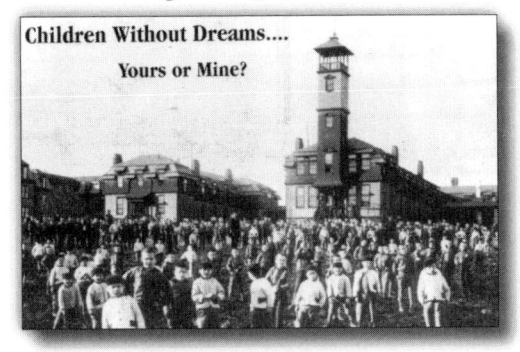

*Mount Loretto Orphanage
Staten Island, New York*

well cared for. The scene in another photo made me weep. It erased any doubts I might have had regarding the call of God on my life—four helpless-looking boys dressed in short pants with suspenders, sleeping under a stairwell of a building in New York, with a caption over the photo reading, *Children without Dreams.*

> ♥ *"Before I formed you in the womb I knew you; before you were born I sanctified you; I ordained you a prophet to the nations"*
> (Jeremiah 1:5).

I left Mount Loretto that day with a grateful heart knowing for sure that God wanted me to inspire brokenhearted children to dream big dreams and reach for the stars. He was going to use my story for His Glory. But, I was only a single mother, without any resources, armed with nothing but conviction and passion to *dare to dream* for these children. The fledgling organization I founded was so young and I had so much to learn. The big question was: *How in the world am I going to be able to accomplish this? And who will help me?*

Part Two

Dare to Dream

The Story of
Dare to Dream
Children's Foundation

Jan Tannyson, Founder

Introduction

"You'll never amount to anything. Look who your parents were!"

Growing up with a foster mother who made degrading statements injuring my self-esteem and not having grandparents, aunts, uncles, or cousins to call or visit me in my foster home made me feel deserted and unwanted. I wondered, *Where is my family? How do I fit in? And who is ever going to love me?*

As a young adult, I wanted to improve myself and was drawn to older people who traveled, read books, ate fine food, and wore beautiful clothing. I had a worldly attitude at that time, and it seemed to me that they were successful and knew a lot more than I did. Listening to their stories fascinated me.

As an older adult, I was determined to start an organization that would make life better for wounded youngsters from fractured families. In 1982 I began visiting youth in group homes and shelters, telling them about my background and how I managed to survive through many difficult situations.

By the grace of God, I founded a non-profit charity in 1987 called "Teenage Profiles for Success" which later became "Dare to Dream Children's Foundation." It has grown because of God bringing people into my life who have embraced the vision to impact our next generation. *Dare to Dream* enables wounded youngsters to recognize their value so they may become people who are capable of fulfilling their destiny.

Chapter Eight

The Start of Something Big

The Right Stuff

As a young adult, I was shy and felt a little rough around the edges. Some of the degrading words spoken over me growing up were imbedded in my personality, and my self-confidence level at social functions was low. In spite of the fact that I grew up in a large home, could play the piano, and had been to the theatre as a child, my feelings of inadequacy were real. Fear of making social mistakes around new people in my life was secretly behind my smiling face.

One evening, while at a wedding, I saw a bowl sitting on an ice sculpture, which I thought was filled with tiny blueberries. When a friend laughed at me and told me that they were actually *caviar*, I wanted to crawl under the table and disappear. This may not have been a big mistake to some people, but I felt really embarrassed.

Feeling uneducated and making social mistakes wasn't helping my self-confidence. So, I watched people at weddings, company banquets, and fine restaurants, who looked like they knew what they were doing—hoping they didn't see me staring at them. A favorite quote from Ann Platz and Susan Wales' book on *Social Graces* states, "Good manners will take one to places money and education cannot buy."

In the early 1980s, I started a business called "Teenage Profiles for Success." My limited knowledge about social skills caused me to design an eight-session course to help teenagers build self-esteem, and not make the same mistakes I made. My first task was to include topics that I wished I would have learned about as a teenager, but didn't. And, since many etiquette courses were already being offered for females, I broke all the rules and pioneered a course for *boys only*.

Experts in their field were invited to teach "The Right Stuff." Topics included—Make the Most of Your Looks, Fitness and Nutrition, Manners Made Easy, Career Goals and Time Management, Conversation Skills, Music and Dance, and How to Dress and Look Your Best. The graduation of my first class of boys was held at the Civic Center in Plano, Texas. Parents were invited to attend an elegant graduation where students were introduced to the audience as if they were the professionals they dreamed about.

"Teenage Profiles for Success" Graduation at the Northwood Country Club, Dallas, Texas

"Ladies and gentlemen, I'd like you to meet Mark, a social worker practicing here in Dallas; next, let's welcome Jake, a Doctor of Internal Medicine"…and so on. The parents, observing their sons' newly found self-assurance, were surprised to find out the *real* dreams of their children. One dad told me, "Jan, I had no idea Robert wanted to be a lawyer."

It was an exciting evening, but what the audience didn't know was that my heart was breaking. Before the graduation, my husband packed his clothes in our car and drove away from our home. That night I wondered, *How will I ever be able to pull this off?* I prayed for strength and God heard my prayer.

To my surprise, at the finale, one of the students walked up to the podium and handed me a dozen red roses. He had no idea how meaningful those flowers were to me at that moment. Precious friends in the audience didn't know that Bill had left, but later expressed to me how composed I was and how beautifully the event flowed.

Although it was hard to keep my spirits high, a few months later, parents encouraged me to include girls in the class, and I agreed. The first co-ed course took place in the *Tennyson Room* at the Sheraton Park Central hotel in Dallas, Texas.

During the "Manners" session, young ladies had the opportunity to express what *turned them off* on a date. The boys had an opportunity to respond by *telling why they would never go out with a particular type of girl*. Students learned how to help a lady with her chair, what to say at a wedding or a funeral, and how to introduce a friend to their parents.

The teenagers loved the excitement of each class, and the parents were thrilled with the results. Subsequent courses took place at Northwood Country Club and the Lincoln Center Hotel in Dallas. My new venture seemed successful and was featured in the March 1984 issue of *Dallas Chamber Magazine*.

Money from Heaven

In 1986, I met a tall, handsome, man at a private party. He was a retired Top Gun Air Force fighter pilot who eloquently told incredible stories of war and its challenges. Although I was impressed with him, he was fascinated with me when I told stories about my childhood. He challenged me to become a professional speaker

"Jan, I've been in Korea, Cambodia, and Vietnam, and I can't imagine what it must have been like to be a displaced child growing up in a home like yours." This man saw qualities in me I never realized. "Why don't you attend the National Speakers Convention next year in Phoenix?" he asked.

"Me, at a speakers convention?" I could no more see myself at a speakers convention than I could see myself flying a fighter jet. But when he told me that some of the greatest speakers in the nation would be there, I wanted to go. Not having the money to cover the airfare and expenses, I prayed, "Lord, if I'm supposed to go to this conference, make a way for it to happen." Not long after that prayer, I walked down the hallway of my home and reached for a book in the bookcase. As I turned the pages, there right before my eyes, were three one hundred-dollar bills! I wondered, *Where did this money come from?* Suddenly, I remembered, that while I was working for a newspaper supplement to the *Dallas Morning News*, I had put the money in a book for a *rainy day*. I had totally forgotten about it, but God hadn't. He waited for just the right moment to direct me to what I called *money from heaven*.

In 1987, I courageously attended the National Speakers Convention in Phoenix, Arizona, and was introduced to prominent speakers from all over the world. I felt like a little girl pressing her nose against the window of a candy store without a clue about how to get inside. Women, dressed beautifully, accessorized with glittering diamonds and pearls, and men, dressed in expensive silk suits, knew exactly what to say, and how and when to say it. I wondered, *Do I really belong here?*

As I scanned the list of speakers and their topics, I chose one that I felt would give me both self-confidence and direction—"If You Want to be a Speaker, What Would You Speak About?"

Barbara Sanfilippo, a lady who had retired from the banking industry, was the speaker. She was wonderful! In the beginning of her career, she had asked herself that same question. After her talk, I came away with the meat of her message—Go to your roots! Go back to where you came from and start there. As I pondered her words I thought, *No thank you! Why would I want to go back to those difficult memories?* Then my thoughts changed

The Start of Something Big

and I wondered, *What would my life have been like if I had been placed in a youth shelter, instead of a foster home? What if I hadn't had someone to put a roof over my head, or give me food to eat?* There were a lot of questions, and I wanted answers.

Once I returned to Dallas, words poured out of me to the administrators of group homes, youth shelters, and detention centers trying to convince them to give me an opportunity to encourage their youth. I explained, "Everyone needs someone to believe in them!"

Discovering that I could *talk straight* to at-risk youth and gain their trust, gave me the confidence to walk into any facility knowing that these youngsters deserved a chance to have a better life. I believe that good seeds planted in young people can change their negative attitudes. One student remarked, "We know you didn't have to come here, but we're glad you did."

Up until this period in time, events for youngsters were predominantly held in Dallas, Texas. However, when I was invited by a former roommate to play at her wedding in Maui, Hawaii, I thought, *Wouldn't it be great to make something wonderful happen in this beautiful place!* During the wedding, I was able to look out the door from the front of the chapel and see the blue ocean waves lapping the shore. Feeling the light grains of sand brushing across my hands as I played the "Hawaiian Wedding Song," I was relishing every moment. Watching the photographer pose the newly married couple on the beach made me wonder if one day I would ever experience a wedding as beautiful as this one.

Jan in Maui, Hawaii

The day after the wedding, I discovered a homeless shelter within a few miles from a heliport where pilots conducted tours of Maui. This triggered me to challenge them to open their doors to these poor youngsters. They took me on a helicopter tour and accepted my idea. The homeless children now had the opportunity to experience the incredible beauty of the waterfalls and amazing sights of the island.

The reality of my circumstances—wanting to keep helping at-risk youth on very limited funds—set in the moment the Texas heat hit me as I exited the plane in Dallas. My brother Gene asked, "Jan, how will you live? You don't have a rich husband or relatives to support you, and the kids you are trying to reach don't have any money to give you."

I responded, "Gene, somehow I just know that I'm doing what I'm supposed to do and I'm not going to worry about it." However, what did concern me was that I lacked a college education. I wondered, *How will I raise money to keep on going?* I began to lose my self-confidence that I could influence adult audiences to help me. But, my military friend, who I had been dating for a few years, interrupted those ideas and told me, "Jan, if you can hold rebellious teenagers in the palm of your hand, you can speak to *any* audience."

At the time, I wasn't familiar with the Biblical scripture when God spoke to Moses, *"Now go; and I will help you speak and will teach you what to say"* (Exodus 4:12). Today, this scripture is a great confidence builder for me.

Practically depleting my saving account to keep things going, I was struggling financially. But now, I realize that finances were just part of my problem; I was also spiritually bankrupt, and needed a stronger faith to proceed. Then, one day in 1987, it finally occurred to me, *Why not start a non-profit organization so people can donate funds to help, and they can get a tax deduction at the same time?* A friend recommended a lawyer, Bob Benson, who helped me apply for non-profit status. We formed a small Board of Directors, and I began speaking at civic clubs to raise funds. The Downtown Exchange Club in Dallas, with the encouragement of one of the members, Mac McRae, said, "We have money in the bank, and I think we should help her." Those significant words gave me the confidence to explore new adventures for some displaced children. The Exchange Club helped me begin this journey from being a single mom with a dream, to a woman with a purpose touching children around the world.

A Mother's Heart and a Soldier's Strength

"Teenage Profiles for Success" was just getting off the ground, but one of life's interruptions caused me to focus in a different direction. Two months before my son's graduation from high school, I received a startling phone call from the principal of Richardson High School telling me that James was not going to graduate.

Shocked, I responded, "I don't understand. My son has good grades and no one has called to tell me differently."

"Mrs. Tennyson, James has been cutting classes, and he has exceeded the limit allowed in order to graduate."

"How could this happen?" I asked.

"Your son has been forging your signature to be excused from his classes."

"That's impossible! James could *never* duplicate my handwriting."

The principal replied, "Well, he must have practiced, because he fooled his teachers, and they released him from his classes." The bottom line was, James wasn't graduating.

A few weeks before all this insanity, an article came out in the *Dallas Morning News* reporting the unique work I was doing with youth through "Teenage Profiles for Success." I was elated by the article, but embarrassed and devastated that my son, whom I dreamed would walk across the stage in a cap and gown, wasn't going to receive a diploma.

During James' senior year, he had a few encounters with the law, but I pushed it off as *senioritis*, believing he was just partying a little more than usual before graduation. One particular Friday evening, I was home alone and received a phone call from the police telling me that they were holding my son at Tom Thumb for breaking the law.

"You need to come here right now," the police officer said.

My heart jumped as I asked, "Is he hurt?"

The officer replied, "He's not hurt, but he and his friend were sniffing aerosol cans trying to get high."

I told him that I would be right there. With my heart beating fast, and my face showing distress, I raced through the door of the store and saw an officer questioning James and his friend about their actions.

The officer asked me, "Do you want him to be taken downtown to the police station?"

I reluctantly said, "Yes, that's where he belongs." After a few hours at the station, he was released to my custody. It was a silent ride back home. James, along with his father and I were required to go to the "First Offender Program" offered by the Dallas Police Department. The parents attended the course in a separate classroom from the offenders as we learned about the consequences of substance abuse on each member of the family. Thinking that everything would be fine after the eight-week program, I was sadly disappointed. Apparently my son hadn't learned his lesson.

The Start of Something Big

A week later a neighbor called to inform me that both of our sons were smoking pot together. Not knowing what to do, I called Cindy, a counselor from the "First Offender Program" to ask for advice. She told me about a local recovery program that had a good track record working with teenagers. After one more incident that involved a blackout, I asked James, "Do you think you have a problem?"

With tears in his eyes, he said, "Obviously."

This moment of recognition was a giant step towards his recovery. I've discovered that unless he admitted that there was a problem, I'd be wasting my time trying to get him help. The following Monday we were interviewed separately with the administrator of Straight, Inc., a recovery program in nearby Richardson. After many hours of conversations with clients and the administrator, I knew this was where James belonged. With fear on his face he pleaded, "Mom, you're not going to leave me here!" Teary-eyed I said, "Yes, I'm your Mom and this is what's best for you." He was devastated. Driving away that afternoon, I felt like I had lost one of my arms.

He attended classes with his peers at Straight during the day, and at night he lived in a host home—another client's residence with a family who were also in the program. This unexpected turn of events flipped my life upside down. When I enrolled my son, I had no idea I might be required to open my home to other boys in the program. When James reached phase two, I was asked to host clients, other than my son, overnight and provide breakfast, a sack lunch, and an evening meal. As far as I was concerned, this was out of the question.

I thought, *How could I, as a single mom, take care of a group of druggie teenagers?* Nevertheless, Straight convinced me this was a vital part of the five-phase program. So, I eventually calmed down and was willing to do whatever it would take to help my son. Rearranging my priorities, "Teenage Profiles for Success" was now put on hold, and I became a host mom instead. Housing as many as eight boys at a time was beyond my comprehension.

During my first night as a host mom, one of the boys tried to cut his wrists with his nails. I later found out that inflicting pain on themselves gave them some kind of weird power surge. My head was screaming, *I can't do this; it's too hard!*

My heart hurt knowing James was not going to be with me on Mother's Day. But, the note that he handed me at the Friday family night meeting is one I will never forget.

Happy Mother's Day. I never thought I would say this, but thank you Mom for putting me here. I can't be with you this Mother's Day, but next year I'll make it the best Mother's Day of your life.

Love, your son, James.

Getting up early, making breakfast, packing lunches, having dinner ready, and doing the laundry for kids who weren't mine, was not easy. Patience and understanding were my daily prayers, as I listened to the boys' stories and dried their tears. Lisa, our daughter, who lived with her father, attended family night once a week to support her brother. The painful look in her eyes showed me how hard this was for her. James finally made second phase, and at that point in the program was permitted to live at home. Each morning, I allowed him to drive his peers to and from the facility in Richardson in my 1965 Mustang convertible for their daily group sessions.

Placing alarms on my windows and doors to alert me if one of the boys decided to run away was something I never dreamed I'd have to do. They slept in a room without a stick of furniture in it, except for wall-to-wall mattresses.

One evening, a teenager whom I trusted that was on the last phase of the program, searched each boy before bedtime. This was to make sure that there wasn't anything in the room that could be used as a weapon on themselves or the other boys. He checked the alarms and removed the batteries, without my knowledge. He escaped through the bedroom window. These types of incidents forced me to have a mother's heart and a soldier's strength to deal with many unpredictable situations over the fourteen months that James was in the program.

In March of 1988, I wrote this note to my sister in Florida:

> *It's getting close to the time that James will be attending his commencement exercises from Straight. He's moving in with Bill as of April 1. So, I'm dealing with an empty nest and have to make some decisions for my life. I have some options: Sell my house and move to the beach; make my home a bed & breakfast; rent a room to a senior citizen; find a good job; rent my house out and become a gypsy; or develop my speaking career and tell my story. A lot of professional speakers tell me that it would be criminal not to tell it. So, I must try to remember what I am grateful for…that way I won't be depressed. I'm at a crossroads and praying to know what God wants me to do. I know if I can just put it in His hands—the right answer will come.*

Having twenty-seven teenagers with some type of alcohol and/or substance abuse problem living in my home was a difficult time for all of our family. However, the payoff for our commitment as a family who stood by James, was to know that he worked the rigid program, and stayed as long as it took to get clean and sober.

On June 3, 1987, we attended his graduation from Straight. Although this was not the graduation celebration I had pictured for my son, I was just as proud as any parent who had ever watched their child walk across a stage wearing a cap and gown. Celebrating James' sobriety each year made me thank God for saving my son's life. After graduation from the program, he moved in with his father. Lisa was away at college and my role as a mother had totally changed.

She Dares to *Dream*

While reading the newspaper one morning, I saw an ad that read: *Family wanting to rent a home near Medical City Hospital*. That gave me an idea. I never thought about renting my home, but I called and made an appointment to meet with the family. Remarkably, when the man arrived at my doorstep, he was the same person who sat next to me at a Bible study a few weeks before! I thought, *This must be a divine appointment*. He came back with his wife and they loved my house. On faith, I had them sign a lease without ever knowing where I was going to live.

Later, I thought, *Jan, you encourage others to dare to dream, so why not live in one of those mansions in the Turtle Creek section of Dallas?* After calling my friend, Gretchen Burns, and telling her I was planning to put an ad in the paper to rent a place, she reminded me of her friend, Betty Baker, who lived alone in Addison, Texas. This woman owned a beautiful home with a swimming pool and spa, which turned out to be exactly what I needed.

Getting rid of nearly all of my possessions, except for the antique mirrors, the baby grand piano, and some of my children's baby toys, I moved into the upstairs level of her home, at an amazingly affordable price. In the front of the house, there was an office with a balcony overlooking the city of Addison; looking out the back, there was a swimming pool and spa. The baby grand looked wonderful in Betty's living room, and the first gathering of *Dare to Dream* volunteers and supporters took place in this lovely setting. This home became the first official *Dare to Dream* office on Palladium, in Addison, Texas.

The Start of Something Big

Focusing on the Dream

I accepted an invitation from a group of seniors from the Internship class at Richardson High School to be the Baccalaureate speaker for their graduation on May 28, 1989. These students had earned the highest grades in their senior class.

The music "Pomp and Circumstance" rang out as the proud students marched into the auditorium wearing their caps and gowns. As I had recently taken a fall and was on crutches, I hobbled across the stage to the lectern, which seemed to take forever.

Looking at the audience into the sea of hopeful faces, out of my heart poured enthusiastic words of wisdom and direction to young men and women on the way to their destiny.

Challenging each of them to reach out to their fellow man and to be committed to high morals, ethics, and values, I encouraged them to seek employment in the world of media and speak up for what they believed was right. At the reception, one parent remarked, "My husband usually falls asleep at these things, but this time, he never missed a word." I considered that quite a compliment. With my heart full of love for the students that day, I left the school and prayed, "Lord, guide and protect each one of these precious young people as they meet the world's challenges to become productive citizens and leaders in our communities."

> ♥ *"Train up a child in the way he should go,*
> *and when he is old he will not depart from it"*
> (Proverbs 22:6).

Discouraging statements spoken to me as a child such as "You're just a foster kid. What makes you think you can do that?" fueled my thinking as an adult to want to create extraordinary experiences for underprivileged youth.

One of my first opportunities came in 1989, when I gave a *Dare to Dream* presentation to children at the National Speakers Convention in Dallas at the Anatole Hotel. This presentation was taped, which now afforded me a recording of my voice with music, which was made available to speakers all over the country.

That same year, I began exploring the possibility of creating a *Dare to Dream* event in the White House. I thought, *Since we pay taxes, that house really belongs to the American people.* So, I put a plan in place. When I learned that Dr. Tim LaHaye, an author, and prominent Bible teacher, was conducting a class in the White House, as well as at Prestonwood Baptist Church right here in Dallas, I wanted to meet him.

One Sunday, I visited his class at Prestonwood, but he wasn't teaching that day. Instead of making a connection concerning a *Dare to Dream* White House event, I viewed a video on a project he and his wife, Beverly, were working on in the jungles of Costa Rica. A team was being recruited from the church to build a house for the teachers of Nicaraguan refugee children who escaped Communism in their country. After the video, the audience was asked to sign up to go on the trip.

"I'd love to go, but right now I don't have the money," I told Tom Lamphere, one of the men promoting the journey. He was surprised at my remark and said, "Jan, think about it. We'll be traveling in shark infested waters and sleeping in tents in a jungle with snakes and mosquitoes as big as your fist. We'll be traveling down waterways with sharks and alligators swimming in the area." Without a clue as to what I was getting into I said, "It sounds like an intriguing adventure to me!" I wasn't a nun traveling to remote parts of the world as I once thought, but I had an adventurous spirit and a willing heart.

After a short conversation he said, "Jan, if you still feel this way next week, call me." The following week I made the call

The Start of Something Big

and assured him, "I'm interested, but as I mentioned before, I'm short on cash." His next words were music to my ears...

"My wife is involved in real estate and has no interest in traveling to the jungle, but she'd love to pay for your trip." My heart danced with joy and within a few weeks I was on my way!

The team flew from Dallas to Belize, to El Salvador and then landed in Costa Rica. After our arrival, we boarded a plane with only four seats and the first group flew to a small runway at the base of the Rio Colorado River. Landing in pouring rain and putting on rubber boots and rain slicks before boarding a long slim canoe with a blue tarp over the top, we cruised down the dangerous river towards a small village of people waiting for us to arrive.

Halfway up the river a team member handed out paper cups to empty out the water that was leaking into our boat. A half-hour later, a small craft in the distance pulled close to ours, and we carefully boarded the new canoe and proceeded down the murky river. This would not have been my *dream* vacation spot—but what an incredible adventure it turned out to be for a lady from New York cruising in the jungles of Costa Rica!

Jan greeting children arriving for school in Costa Rica

Smiling villagers waving and shouting, "The Americans are coming! The American's are coming!" was an incredible sight to see as we drew closer to the shore. Inhabitants of all ages and sizes happily greeted each of us as we stepped out of the boat. Setting up our folding cots in the open-air building with mosquito netting to protect ourselves, was our first undertaking as we prepared to spend the evening.

The next day a group of precious children arrived by canoe from a village upstream to attend school. Helping the little ones out of the boat, I warmly greeted each boy and girl and took their small hands as I guided them to the shore.

Speaking in a simple classroom with long tables and chairs, the children attentively listened to my *dare to dream* message. Two team members, a nurse and a translator joined me during the thirty-minute session.

Picture a small hut filled with villagers in this tropical jungle setting singing hymns as I softly played my battery-operated keyboard. It was a glowing candlelight atmosphere, and I wished this evening would never end. Heaven orchestrated this moment in time that ignited a spark in my spirit for bringing music to the people wherever God would send me. This amazing memory turned out to be my first mission trip—when I didn't even know what a mission trip was.

Jan speaking to children from Nicaragua in a village in Costa Rica

The day when I walked into Prestonwood Baptist Church searching for Dr. LaHaye, I pictured myself all dressed up sitting at a baby grand piano in the White House, wearing a sparkling beaded gown and speaking to dignitaries, supporters, and youngsters from the Washington D.C. area. Instead, I found myself wearing muddy boots lifting the spirit of children in a jungle. God had His plan and was resurrecting my love for missions work in faraway places.

Sitting next to me on the airplane back home, I shared my dream with a team member, Leonard Robertson, who was an accountant. "Can you think of a much worse situation for a kid than trying to get along in this crazy world without a parent's love or direction? There's a crowd of young people facing this every day." He listened as I continued to share my concerns. "Many youngsters wind up in shelters, detention centers, and eventually, in prison. I want to help them, but I don't know where to start."

He referred me to a lawyer in Dallas, Steve Gillis, who helped me reinstate my non-profit status. He became a board member, and has remained as an advisory board member. In October 1987, without much money or staff, "Teenage Profiles for Success" was established as a 501(c) 3 non-profit organization, and eventually became Dare to Dream Children's Foundation.

♥ *"A man's heart plans his way, but the Lord directs his steps"*
(Proverbs 16:9)..

The Dream Takes Wings

The YMCA Casa de los Amigos youth shelter that is now a Salvation Army shelter in Dallas was the first youth facility I visited when I returned home from the National Speakers Convention in 1987. The Director saw my heart and gave me permission to talk with their youth. Sharing my story and encouraging the youngsters to never give up on their dreams, I quickly captured their attention. Before finishing my talk, I quoted words from Mary Crowley's tiny blue book—*Be Somebody ...God didn't take time to make a nobody.*

At first it was difficult to share my faith in the center because a staff member objected to any talk about *God* and wanted to close the door on me. However, the youth director, Jimmie Slater, who eventually became a board member with *Dare to Dream*, vouched for me and said, "Our young people are hearing everything else, why not Jan's program?" Ultimately, they asked me to return. Jimmie later stated at a meeting, "The trunk of Jan's car became her office where

She Dares to Dream

Jan with a youth from a shelter on the Texas Queen Riverboat

she kept a cardboard file box and a keyboard. She'd knock on our door, introduce herself to our kids, and tell them her story. There was no doubt about her sincerity. She gave our kids hope as she encouraged them to dream. They loved her."

In May 1990, Lee Schimmell, Executive Director of Promise House, a shelter for homeless, runaway, and at-risk teens, wrote me a letter stating:

Your Dare to Dream concept in exposing youth to what could be possible for their lives, has helped our youngsters to strive for and achieve a better future.

That same week, I went to City Hall and changed the name from Teenage Profiles for Success to *Dare to Dream*.

Continuing conducting classes at facilities that worked with at-risk youth, I developed relationships with the Dallas County Juvenile System, Texas Youth Commission, Buckner Children's Home, YMCA Casa Shelter, and many others. Wherever I traveled, doors were open to the *dare to dream* message. Wanting to conduct some classes in *dream* settings, I built relationships with the staff on the Texas Queen Riverboat on Lake Ray Hubbard, the Sea Dream yacht in Florida, the Million-Air aviation facility in Addison, Texas, as well as with luxury hotels, restaurants, and penthouses.

Whenever I traveled out of Texas to New York, Florida, Louisiana, California, Idaho, and overseas, I searched out agencies where youth needed encouragement. My family in Florida, New York, and California didn't quite understand

The Start of Something Big

what I was doing and wondered, *What is she up to now? Can't she just relax? She'll go up and talk to anyone.* Being driven to make things happen for kids who couldn't speak up for themselves wasn't always the popular thing to do. But, it was worth it.

> ♥ *"Behold, children are a heritage from the Lord, the fruit of the womb is a reward. Like arrows in the hand of a warrior, So are the children of one's youth"*
> (Psalm 127:3-4).

My Last Call

In 1991, the people who were renting my house moved out, and the lady I was living with got married, so I decided to move back into my own home. Since I didn't know if God wanted me to move back permanently, I put a quilt on the floor of my bedroom along with a pillow and a sheet, and slept on the floor for almost three months. I told myself, *In other countries people sleep on the floor all the time, so why not me?* I went to the dollar store and purchased one place setting, a fork, knife, and spoon and each day asked God, "Do you want me to stay here? Do you want me to sell this house?" I wasn't clear on the answer. I put one book in the bookcase, one set of towels in the bathroom, and little by little, my home was starting to take shape.

While taking my morning walk, I passed a store that sold bedroom furniture and fell in love with a beautiful white wrought iron bed. I made my first large purchase, which began the total restoration of my home.

Still committed to the *Dare to Dream* mission, in 1991 I put up a card table in my bedroom with a telephone on it. But, in order for people to take me seriously, I needed a professional office. For almost a year, I contacted real estate owners in Dallas, and was turned down over and over.

In 1992, totally frustrated, I decided to make one more call. But first, I had a conversation with God. "Lord, this is my last call. If something doesn't happen this time, I'll use that as a message that you want me doing something else." I dialed the number and a woman answered.

"Hello, may I help you?"

I replied, "My name is Jan Tennyson, and I'm searching for donated office space to help at-risk youth in Dallas. Most of them have been abused, neglected, and end up in foster care or detention centers. I want to create programs to give them hope." She listened quietly. Frustrated, I said, "If you don't want to help me, that's fine; I can do something else—this is God's work anyway."

She interrupted and asked, "You're a Christian? I hesitated for a moment and answered, "Yes, a very discouraged Christian."

She responded, "Hold on, I have an idea. I'll call you in a few days." I thought, *Wow! This is the first time someone sounds like they might want to help me.* A few days later my phone rang, and she asked me to meet her at a building on Steppington at Meadow and Central Expressway in Dallas. Inviting me up the back staircase, she offered me a small office with one window at the end of the building. I looked around and graciously accepted it. But, having no enthusiasm to put a desk or a telephone in the space told me *this isn't it*. Instead, I used the room to store some *Dare to Dream* T-shirts.

A few weeks later, she phoned me again asking me to meet her in front of the same building, wanting to show me a different office. I had high expectations and when I arrived, we went into the *front* entrance and walked up to the second floor. Opening the door to a large corner office with windows on two sides she asked, "Will this work for you?"

Without hesitation, I exclaimed, "Absolutely, this is wonderful!" Noticing there was an adjoining room with lots of telephone equipment that needed to be removed, I asked, "If I gathered a group of volunteers to clean out this room, would you be willing to let me use this space as well?" She cautiously responded, "Yes, as long as it doesn't cost us any money." Agreeing to pay utilities to the Independent Order of Forresters, they blessed us with nearly 2,000 square feet of donated office space including a storage room and a reception area for seven years!

In 1999, The Forresters needed their space back and asked us to move. I prayed about God's direction and said that if He wanted this organization to continue, by faith, I wanted Him to provide another donated office. A few months later, a church member graciously offered donated space in DeSoto, Texas. Because a local secretary was considering working with us, we moved some furniture to that location. But, her plans changed, and it was too far for me to drive back and forth from DeSoto, especially considering the late hours I was working. Consequently, the Board of Directors encouraged me to keep a *Dallas* location.

I worked out of my home for several months until a Board member found a new location just south of Mockingbird on Central Expressway. In November 2000, after much prayer, I signed a lease at 5401 N. Central Expressway, Suite 320, Dallas, Texas 75205. Our 750 square feet of space turned out to be exactly what we needed. God blessed the space, and we remained there for the next seven years.

In 2007, we moved to our present location at 6310 LBJ Freeway, Suite 111, Dallas, Texas 75240.

> ♥ *"Let us not be weary in doing good, for at the proper time we will reap a harvest if we do not give up"*
> (Galatians 6:9 NIV).

Chapter Nine

The Children Are Our Future

I have often been asked, "Jan, why do you do what you do? There's not a lot of appreciation or money in speaking to at-risk youth. What keeps you going?" Perhaps this chapter will help answer these questions.

Straight from the Kids

- "My sister and I were sitting at the kitchen table while Mom was preparing breakfast. Dad was drunk the night before, and when he came downstairs, he yelled, 'What's all the noise about?' With a frightened look, Mom said, 'We'll be quiet, the kids are just getting ready for school.' He took out a gun and shot Mom in the head right in front of us."

- "One night my sister took her twin babies to bed with her. She was on drugs, and didn't realize she was lying on top of one of them. The baby smothered to death during the night."

- "My parents gave me my first drugs."

- "My Dad is gone; my Mom's in jail and my Grandmother's in jail too. I guess that's why I'm in jail today."

- "I want to go home, but I can't because Dad gets drunk and beats me."

- A young man with no remorse said, "I sold my Mom's wedding ring for drugs."

During my talk at Covenant House in Florida, a refuge for homeless youth, it was obvious the kids looked up to a tall male teenager in the audience who was covered with tattoos. After my talk I asked, "What's your name?" He answered, "Spider. People are afraid of spiders."

I responded, "Should I be afraid of you?" He said, "*You* can call me Ray." We had lunch and talked for about an hour. I encouraged him, "You know Ray, you have some real leadership qualities, and I believe some day you could be a teacher right here at this shelter."

He answered, "Really? Nobody ever said anything like that to me before." For the first time, he wanted to do something positive with his life.

Parents—I encourage you to listen to this boy's heart.

"I told my mother, who was half mesmerized reading the paper with her fifth glass of wine, 'I'll be in late, I'm going to a midnight movie with my friends.' Dad was away on a business trip and I knew I had a golden opportunity to do my thing. I planned to go to the movie, but on the way I met some friends who were going to a party. They were on a beer run and asked me to join them. The choice was mine, and I made the wrong call. The oldest in the group went in the liquor store and ordered a couple of cases of beer. They never even checked his I.D. Boy did we put one over! The party was in full swing.

Smoking some pot and having a few beers was fun, and when the best looking girl at the party asked me to dance, I really fit in. One thing led to another and before the night was over I was totally drunk. A friend wanted to drive me home, but I knew I could handle it.

"Mom was still up when I got home. She was annoyed because it was obvious that I had too much to drink. I can hardly remember going to bed that night.

"The next morning I didn't even know where my car was parked. I had a total blackout. She didn't question me about the evening—she trusted me. Little did she know I could have died that night. How I wish she would have asked me about the movie and checked it out. I needed her to be strong and to hold me accountable for my actions. I walked all over her and she never knew the difference. If I had one thing I would tell her, it would be… 'Mom … don't drink! It's hard out there today to make the right decisions. Peer pressure is killing me. I need you to hold me accountable for my actions. If you can't control your alcohol, how can I? I'm only a kid.'"

Another question I am frequently asked is, "What difference does it make to speak to troubled youth only one time? Because they move from home to home through *the system*, you may never see them again." My answer simply is this: Just as employees, church congregations, and college students move around, they aren't prevented from listening to a keynote speaker one time, with the possibility that it might improve the quality of their lives. Are our youth worth any less? Shouldn't our most vulnerable youngsters have the same opportunities?

Creating educational and motivational experiences for at-risk youth can be challenging. Asking folks to allow these youngsters into their boardrooms, yachts, restaurants, etc. is sometimes shocking. People are a little apprehensive when they find out the youth have either been locked up, or may be going down the wrong road of life. When I convince people that I am offering them an opportunity to change the direction of the lives of these youngsters, it ends up being a win-win situation.

Teaching elementary life-skills might seem simple to you and me, but it is a life-changing experience to displaced youngsters who dropped out of school. Many don't know how to address a letter, or where to put the stamp on an envelope. Some are about to live life on their own, and still can't read a book or write a check. Teaching them about having a bank account and making a budget for expenses is new information. Through creative programming, *Dare to Dream* picks up the broken pieces of their lives and gives them the help they need.

One teenager in a shelter told me "I came into this room hating the world, wanting to hurt people. Now I love the world and want to help people. Thank you for being here."

One successful young man who loves the Lord wrote, "I'm the man I am today because of what I learned in one of your Teenage Profiles for Success classes. Thank you for what you do." *Dare to Dream* doesn't receive many notes like that, but it is always a joy to know that a life was touched because someone cared.

> ♥ *"Blessed is the man who perseveres under trial, because when he has stood the test, he will receive the crown of life that God has promised to those who love Him"*
> (James 1:12 NIV).

An Evening with the Stars

Dare to Dream needed recognition to get the financial support to sustain my vision to inspire and impact the lives of troubled youth. Not having many resources, I prayed, "Lord, if you want me to move forward with this work, please give me an idea when I wake up tomorrow morning, that will let me know, this thought must be from God." Remarkably, the next morning in August 1992, my heart whispered—*put on a concert at the Meyerson this year.* I questioned, "The Meyerson? Are you sure?" The Meyerson is one of the greatest concert halls in the world. The thought was so strong; I had no doubt about what I was supposed to do. The next day, I visited the magnificent concert hall in downtown Dallas, Texas, and made my plea to the planning director.

"I'd like to book a date for a concert to benefit *Dare to Dream.*"

Without hesitation he remarked, "Jan, any worthwhile date this year is already taken. How about next year?"

I persisted and said, "No, it has to be *this* year. What's happening the week between Christmas and the New Year?"

He responded, "Nobody wants that week; we seldom book anything during that time."

I answered, "Terrific! That means that it's available. Would you pencil us in for the twenty-eighth of December?"

He paused for a moment and said, "Yes, we can do that."

I told him, "I don't have any money to give you right now, but when the time comes for the deposit, I'll have what you need."

"Jan, we believe you. What will you name the concert and who will be on stage?"

"I'm going to call it 'An Evening With the Stars.'"

"That's a great name. Who are the stars?"

By faith I said, "I don't know yet, but I promise, the show will be spectacular." With a dream and a prayer, without a penny to spend, or a performer in mind, a date was booked at the Morton H. Myerson Symphony Center, and God did the rest.

The next day I prayed for inspiration to know who should be on stage. The first person I thought of was my talented friend, Linda Septien, an amazing singer who can sing from Bach to Broadway with style. When I found out she was pregnant, and her baby's due date was close to the date of the show, I was happy for her but surprised that she accepted the invitation to perform and direct the show!

Since the concert would take place during the Christmas Season, I didn't have to think twice when I selected a pianist from my list of entertainers. His name was Klaus Kluen. Today, he is one of the top worship leaders in the nation. He accepted my invitation, and suggested I meet another incredibly talented vocalist—W.T. Greer, who was singing at the Melrose Hotel in Dallas. After listening to his rich, vibrant voice, I invited him to join our show. He was delighted to accept my invitation.

It was already August, and there was a lot of work to be done. With little knowledge on how to create an event, I went to a local TV station for help. I was told, "Jan, you have to make your request at least a year in advance for us to do anything."

I responded, "I don't have that kind of time. You've heard my story, now do what you think is right." I left the room praying that they would have a sympathetic heart towards my request. Some time later, the station surprised me by setting up a series of public service announcements weeks before our event.

The day of our concert had arrived—December 28, 1992. Excitement was at a peak as youngsters entered the impressive lobby. This extraordinary building is named in honor of Morton H. Meyerson, the former president of Electronic Data Systems (EDS). People from all walks of life viewed our giant display of *Dare to Dream* events displayed in the lobby outside the concert hall. Groups of youngsters from local shelters and group homes were escorted to box seats—the most expensive seating in the house. Perhaps for the first time in their lives, these abused, neglected and foster children were treated like royalty. Homeless men and women temporarily living in an inner-city shelter were provided selected seats in the orchestra section. Pastors from area churches were also blessed with complimentary seats.

Youth from a Dallas Shelter attend a Dare to Dream event at the Morton H. Meyerson Symphony Center in 1992.

The centerpiece of the Meyerson is the Eugene McDermott concert hall named after the co-founder of Texas Instruments. Every detail was designed to attain the highest acoustical quality. Heads turned as guests admired the amazing 2,062-seat theatre. The audience was seated and the performance was about to begin!

The opening lines of the show were written in a note to me from a teenager who lived at a girl's home in Idaho. A child's voice rang out in the dark concert hall—

> "I was alone and afraid in a world I never made. I closed my eyes and dared to dream. I dreamed of a world of laughter and bright smiling faces. When I opened my eyes, all I could see were sad and hardened faces. It was then I realized, those are the faces of laughter with just a little help."

The lights slowly came up as Linda Septien stepped out of the shadows and sang "Somewhere" from the Broadway show "West Side Story." The words in this song expressed my heart for the children—*There's a place for us, a time and place for us. Hold my hand and we're halfway there. Hold my hand and I'll take you there Somehow, Some day, Somewhere!*

I invited my pastor, Dr. Morris Sheats from Hillcrest Church, to give a message to the audience that was straight from my heart.

He said, "This is truly an *Evening With The Stars*. And the stars, my dear people, are sitting right in your seat. We are on the threshold of a New Year and you have the opportunity to let your light shine brightly." He added, "The stars are always shining; even behind the clouds, the stars are always there. Through the storms of life, God is always there. As you leave this concert hall tonight, let your star shine brightly before men; that people will know that you have been touched by the hand of God."

After he finished his talk, I was in awe, as Ann Quest, the leader of the Dallas Prayer Ministry (now called the Greater Dallas Prayer Ministry), walked out on the stage and presented me with a radiant, beveled glass star. The concert was outstanding and the presence of God reigned throughout the Meyerson that evening.

Financially, we broke even, but the unexpected publicity was the springboard that propelled *Dare to Dream* towards becoming a respected, worthy ministry that has encouraged literally thousands of children around the world.

> ♥ *"Let your light so shine before men, that they may see your good works and glorify your Father in heaven"*
> (Matthew 5:16).

Shining Lights

Citizens from every walk of life who have been transformed by the love of Christ are given the opportunity to volunteer and share what life was like before and after they invited Jesus into their hearts. Hundreds of wounded youth are hearing amazing testimonies, which gives them hope for a brighter future. *Dare to Dream* is here today because of people who join me in my quest to establish an organization that will stand alongside youth who need someone and something to believe in.

With fond and precious memories I honor those volunteers who have passed on to their eternal reward: Audrey Holley, Al Messinger, Mike Totin, Jan Swerske, Robert Louis, and Jay McLure.

From the bottom of my heart, I thank those who were our first Board Members: Robert Benson, Jan Doleh, Howard Pierson, Leonard Robertson, Steve Gillis, Gretchen Burns, Jim White, Mike Langton, and Zora Burkleo. Years later, Larry Gardner, Lisa Barnham, Becky Craft, Don Dowell, Tony Lissota, Pam Baxter, Joan Moore, Stella Naifeh, Merritt Westbrook, Steve Wilschetz, Pamela Bolton, Jimmy Slater, Jim Ash, Ollie Malone, Lynn Sinclair, and Dennis Allen joined us. I thank the numerous people who have served on our Board and Advisory Board throughout the years.

To the churches, corporations, civic clubs, associations, individuals, and children who have prayerfully and financially contributed to sustain our ministry, I am sincerely grateful. Don Dowell introduced *Dare to Dream* to one of the many organizations that stood by our side during some very tough times—the Building Owners and Managers Association (BOMA). I appreciate the efforts of all those who served on the Community Outreach Committee.

On the pages that follow are photos of some of our *Shining Lights* who have inspired our youth and have volunteered with *Dare to Dream* Children's Foundation:

She Dares to Dream

Some of our 2003 Volunteers

Back row left to right: Andi Knowles, Jim & Dale Ash, Carole Bond, Eric Douglas, Steve Colbert, Tony Lisotta, Rev. Jimmie Slater, James Patsellis, Tony Vera, Mike Totin, Jay Mclure, Marsha Allen, and Brett Martin. Front row: David Abboud, Kay Jones, Dallas' Assistant Police Chief, Randy Hampton, Jan Tennyson, Suzanne Sutherland, Geri Kihlberg, and Nolan Mills.

Some of our 2005 Volunteers

Standing left to right: Rev. Ricky Texada, Tony Vera, Kay Jones, John Patton, Lisa Walker, Suzanne Sutherland, Virginia Reynolds, Bill Kushnir, Pamela Bolton, John Frances, Shirley Kaczka, Lynn Sinclair Judy Messinger, Betty Griffith, Geri Kihlberg, Steven Colbert, Steve Hammer, and James Patsellis. Seated: Jay McLure, Ollie Malone, Dannine Nesbitt, David Abboud, Jan Tennyson, Nicole Reynolds, Anne Snelling, Tabatha Bratcher, and Jansi Kelley.

The Children Are Our Future

A Volunteer Rally at Jan Tennyson's home 2007

Seated back row left to right: Donna Austin, Kay Jones, Dan & Sara Lenhart
Standing: Jim Fant, guest, and Cassandra Silvester.
Seated: Linda Deskin, Marsha Allen, and Jay McLure.
Front row: Jan Tennyson, Lisa Walker, Pamela Bolton and Lynn Sinclair.

Some of our 2009 Volunteers

Back row left to right: Frank Hurtado, Tony Vera, John Heusinkveld,
Travis Wortham, Dan Lenhart, Jim Hagan, Ted Cole, Donna Slater,
Harold Wilson, Board member-Jimmy Slater, and Marsha Allen
Second Row: Sheri Buckingham, Ignace Zidor, Armeda Jost, Jan Tennyson, Sarah
Lenhart, Dorcas Kameri, Carolyn Stehr, Jacque Leonard, Jim and Dale Ash,
Front Row: Suzanne Sutherlnd, Lisa Walker, Maria Reyes, Mark Brooks,
Allan Buckinham, Barbie Cordier, and Board member-Dennis Allen.

Some 2009 volunteers not pictured: Don & Judy Adaire, Gretchen Burns, Gay Darden-Carver, James Butler, Valerie Butler, Crew Dykes, Eric Flyg, Homer Freeman, Jack Gammon, Wayne Johnson, Paul Kramer, Gene Little, Clifford Mitchell, Judy & Charlie Pollinzi, Michelle Ross, David Russell, Della Sowunmi, Todd Thomas, and Virginia Tuggy.

Other volunteers from past years include: Chris Andry, Ed Aston, John Ayo, Gary Billips, Dee Blackerby, Tony Buchannan, Bill Buntyn, Tom Carlson, Allen Clark, Eric & Darla Calloway, Carole Crabtree, Mauricio Cornejo, Shreya Dabholka, Delisa Day, Maria Drunhorn, Jay Duke, Shawna Dunnaway, Amber Edmunds, Sharon Edmunds, Rich Esselstrom, Cassie Fausett, Donna Flemming, Dave Gerow, Randall & Paula Graber, Jacqueline Hill, Francisco Martinez, Richard Hilton, Brett Hoff, Charlotte Holland, Gregg Kennemir, Kim LeCompte, Ed Lozano, Dr. Louis Mejia, Rick Moore, Adam Morris, Donna Muldrew, Jerry Nash, Donna Nix, Sal Ocha, Kelly Furlong-Osmond, Angelo Palacio, Ken Parks, Wayne Patrick, Rita Paul, Chris Plekenpol, Gabriel Ponce, Mary Ponder, David Pager, Virginia Reynolds, Sherry Riehn, Sharon Schobe, Connie Stanton, Elise Stark, William Thomas, Harry Traywick, Lorri Trimmer, Shani Underwood, John Upton, Carla Williams, and Mary Vogds.

I also appreciate the many groups who have helped me personally and professionally—Fellowship of Professional Women (FPW) www.fpwdallas. org, the women who meet weekly at Connie Tolbert's Bible study in Dallas, and the ladies of the Heritage Ranch Bible Study in Fairview, Texas.

If you served *Dare to Dream* in some way and did not see your name in this book, know your contribution was valuable because you touched the lives of youngsters who will touch our future.

♥ *"Speak up for those who cannot speak for themselves, for the rights of all who are destitute. Speak up and judge fairly; defend the rights of the poor and needy"* (Proverbs 31:8, 9 NIV).

Triumph of the Human Spirit

One day, as I was looking into a sea of despondent faces of ten to seventeen-year-old males in a detention center, I asked, "How many of you *never* had someone pray for you one-on-one?" Three quarters of the audience of fifty raised their hands. Standing in front of the room, our team of volunteers waited for the youth to come up for prayer. For the first couple of minutes, no one moved; then, one by one, boys slowly walked up and emptied their hearts. Teardrops flowed down their cheeks as volunteers prayed blessings over each of them. That evening, they experienced the love and compassion of people who were the hands and feet of Jesus to a very hurting generation.

Pamela Bolton, a volunteer and former *Dare to Dream* Board member, gave a message to youth one evening at a juvenile detention center encouraging them to think about their future: "Picture a tombstone with the year of your birth on it, and a dash with an empty space after it. What will the pages of your life story read between now and the day you die?"

We can't control the date of our birth or the date of our death, but we can control what happens in between. Challenging at-risk youth to change their attitude and their behavior is essential to deterring crime in our cities.

Another important arm of *Dare to Dream* is to share our years of experience and encourage young ministries to persevere through the storms that come our way.

One sweet woman, with a vision to minister to the elderly, visited my office in Dallas with her mother. She later wrote:

> *We came away daring to expand our vision of what is possible. We reinforced our belief that God will reach those in difficulty with the hope of His Word; that His comfort will be carried to those confined due to illness or age and that others who share this dream will partner with us as we dare to walk in obedience and faith into God's dream made reality.*
>
> Shades of Grace Ministries
Natalie Grace Nichols
Nacogdoches, Texas

One volunteer, after observing a *Dare to Dream* session with youth from a homeless shelter at the Million-Air facility in Addison, Texas, said with tears in her eyes, "Jan, this is truly *triumph of the human spirit*. The hopeless looking faces of the youngsters, when they first arrived here, have turned to smiles; now they have a desire to contribute to society and achieve their dreams. I'm so glad I was here to see this transformation right before my eyes."

I realize today that this session was inspired, not by the human spirit, but by the inspiration of the Holy Spirit.

> ♥ *"The Spirit of the Lord God is upon me, Because the Lord has anointed me to preach good tidings to the poor; He has sent me to heal the brokenhearted, To proclaim liberty to the captives, and the opening of the prison to those who are bound"*
> (Isaiah 61:1).

Chapter Ten

Divine Appointments

Mary Kay Ash

For years I admired Mary Kay Ash because she believed in God, family, and then career—in that order. The first time I met her was in 1986, as the guest of a friend who was invited to a party at her home in Dallas. We drove up and a valet parked the car. Surprised to see Mary Kay opening the door and greeting each one personally, her warm welcome made me feel as though she had known me for years.

Once the guests arrived, we had refreshments and later enjoyed a tour of her home. Being a pianist, I had a hard time keeping my hands off the piano in the living room.

"Do you play?" I asked Mary Kay.

She nodded her head at me and sat down at the black *player* piano. Carefully placing her hands on the keys, they mechanically moved up and down. She smiled and remarked, "I play pretty well, don't you think?" We both laughed.

Two years later, in June 1988, I had a unique idea on how I wanted to spend my birthday. I picked up the phone and called Mary Kay Cosmetics headquarters in Dallas, Texas. Her personal secretary answered.

"Hello, my name is Jan Tennyson. I'm the Founder of Teenage Profiles for Success here in Dallas. I'd like to celebrate my birthday in July at your headquarters by inviting Mary Kay to tell her story to a group of displaced teenagers from a youth shelter." I also asked to use one of the training rooms for the party.

"That sounds interesting," she remarked.

After discussing the idea with Mary Kay, all of my requests were granted, including a tour of the facility!

The special day arrived. Watching the large van filled with smiling teenage girls pull up in front of the building made me believe that this was going to be a day to remember. The faces of the girls, between the ages of ten and sixteen, pressing their noses against the windows, were filled with expectancy. Excitement mounted as they walked through the grand lobby with its marble floors and tall windows.

"Where is Mary Kay?" one girl asked. I explained to the group that Mary Kay would visit us in one of the classrooms in about thirty minutes. Arriving at the training room, the teenagers mingled with one another, looking towards the doorway from time to time, hoping to get a glimpse of the guest of honor. I called the girls to attention and asked them to take their seats.

Introducing myself, I told the girls that it was my birthday, and as a special present for all of us, I invited Mary Kay to tell us about her life. I explained, "You may be surprised to learn that she didn't always have it as easy as you might think." I told them that she would be arriving in about fifteen minutes; but first, I would like to share some of my story and why I started *Dare to Dream*. Getting their full attention after mentioning that I grew up in foster care, the girls knew I understood their hard times and could connect with their situations.

"When Mary Kay comes through that door, let's give her a roaring standing ovation. Pretend your seats are spring-loaded, and jump to your feet, clapping and cheering as loud as you'd like." That must have sounded like fun, because the group was smiling from ear to ear.

Mary Kay Ash on Jen Tennyson's Birthday 1988

The special moment arrived! The doors in the back of the room slowly opened, and there she was—the queen of the cosmetic world, looking beautiful in her dark green and black-checkered suit. With the girls cheering her on as she walked down the center aisle, Mary Kay remarked, "My, my, this is better than the Miss America pageant."

Arriving at the front of the room, she handed me a gift basket filled with Mary Kay products and told me what a pleasure it was to be with the girls. She wished me a very Happy Birthday and pinned a beautiful pink silk corsage on my white suit jacket. It felt like a mom presenting a daughter with a flower at her graduation.

I announced to the girls, "This great company began in September, 1963. With her life savings of only a few thousand dollars, and the help of one of her children, a now-grown son, Richard Rogers, she started the long process of making her dreams become a reality for her and the millions of women across America. She had a dream that to most people might have seemed impossible. But, her company, with God's help, makes dreams come true. And now, it is my pleasure to introduce a woman I truly admire, Mary Kay Ash."

Once the applause subsided, she looked into the faces of her young audience and told the girls, "I had to take care of my father from childhood. He had tuberculosis and remained an invalid and in need of a great deal of tender, loving care. My mother was the sole support of our family and had to work long hours. So I had to do a lot of things on my own. I had to keep house, cook meals, and go to school. My mother always told me, "You can do it."

I became a Christian when I was seven years old. A Psalm from the Bible that gave me great comfort during some difficult times is Psalm 34:4. *"I sought the Lord and He heard me and delivered me from all my fears.'"*

When she finished her talk, she asked one of her staff to give each girl a small heart necklace with a mustard seed inside. I interrupted, and asked, "Mary Kay, would you be willing to personally hand the heart to each girl?"

She smiled and answered, "Of course, why didn't I think of that?" The girls lined up around the room, and before she placed the gift in their hand, she asked each one, "How are you?" With hesitation, most responded, "Fine." She encouraged them to change their words. "Say you're great! Whether or not you feel it or not, say great! Pretty soon you'll feel that way. If you don't think you're great, nobody else will."

After our session with the girls, I told Mary Kay that I wanted to write my autobiography but didn't know where to start. She encouraged me. "Jan your story will be an inspiring book. Start by writing a table of contents and then work from there." Before leaving the room, she added, "Jan, after the tour, I'd like you and your guests to join me in my office." I was surprised and delighted!

After she said goodbye to the girls in the training room, the teenagers toured the manufacturing plant. Watching bottles, cosmetics, perfumes and lotions moving down the assembly line was captivating. The class observed products being produced, boxed, and on their way to shipping. I told the group, "This company will be around a long time, and has a lot to offer anyone who wants to get ahead, regardless of their circumstances."

As the youngsters boarded the vans, a staff member from one of the shelters thanked me for sharing my birthday with her girls. Watching the youngsters board the vans, I couldn't help but think how wonderful it would be if some of these girls became high-powered sales women with Mary Kay Cosmetics.

My guests and I walked back into the grand lobby and were escorted up to Mary Kay's office. We boarded the luxurious elevator and felt as if we were in a Hollywood scene in a movie. The rooms were beautifully decorated in pink and white and the bathroom had the most fabulous gold leaf mirror I had ever seen. Mary Kay cordially welcomed us to her office and said, "Jan, I'm proud of what you are doing for these young women. You are planting seeds of greatness while there is still time to grow." I truly appreciated those words, coming from a woman I greatly respected and admired.

Standing close to her desk, I noticed a fish bowl and asked about it. She explained that once a salesperson reaches her financial goal, she brings back her mustard seed and places it in the fishbowl.

"How wonderful," I responded. I felt like a princess sitting in court with the Queen. Meeting and speaking with one of the most famous ladies in the world and having a *Dare to Dream* event for some very unfortunate youngsters, will always be a day to remember. What a great 48th birthday present!

> ♥ *"...If you have the faith as a mustard seed, you will say to this mountain, move from here to there, and it will move; and nothing will be impossible for you"*
> (Matthew 17:20)..

Three Different Women, Three Different Worlds

During the summer of 1990, three young women who grew up in the same foster home—Peggy, my sister from Florida, Rose (Cookie), my foster sister from Turkey and I, were visiting New York City at the same time. We hadn't planned to be there together, but once we connected, I suggested that the three of us meet in the lobby of the Foundling Home, the agency where we were placed as youngsters. They agreed that it was a fabulous idea!

The eventful day arrived. Peg and I walked into the lobby at the same time, and Cookie arrived shortly after. With open arms, we ran to each other and the three of us embraced. We were so glad to see one another. The administrator came out smiling and said, "It's wonderful when people like you come back to share your stories with our girls." Inviting us into a living room at one of the dorms, we met a group of tough looking young mothers, between the ages of fifteen and twenty-five; some were holding their babies. The bored look on their faces as they slouched on the coaches throughout the room, told me that they weren't much interested in having visitors. It was obvious they had lived fast lives and needed understanding and encouragement. However, after telling my story and discovering that the three of us were all former foster children, their demeanor changed. They hung onto every word we said.

Cookie shared a different message than mine. Noticing that most of the teens were runaways, rebellious, and pregnant, she totally surprised me when she asked, "What about next time? Will the same thing happen again?" She expressed the tragic situation of bringing babies into a world when they don't have parents who are healthy enough to take care of them. She was angry, and told them that all three of us had personally experienced the devastation of not having a solid family to call our own. The girls were glued to her words.

Peggy was shy about sharing, but was willing to give some encouraging words. I urged the girls to do what is possible and let God handle the impossible. I said, "We may never meet again, but one day you can do the same thing we are doing. Encourage one another to experience God's best for your lives. Go back to school. Practice good manners, and don't use foul language. Believe in the God that believes in you and your life will change." I concluded our time with a prayer, asking God to help us forgive those who have hurt us. The young moms had a total attitude change and promised to pray and *dare to dream*.

Uniting as foster sisters who loved one another was a powerful message for the girls to experience.

For years I had created special events for young people, but that day in New York was the first time I had an opportunity to create something spectacular for *my* family. Peggy and Cookie's eyes almost popped out when they walked outside the Foundling and saw a fabulous gray stretch limousine parked at the curb waiting for them. Cookie yelled, "I don't believe it!" Peg smiled and said, "Leave it to Jan." As we pulled up to St. Patrick's Cathedral, one of our favorite sights in New York City, people stopped and looked to see who was getting out of the limousine. We stepped out feeling like royalty arriving at a wedding.

Peggy, Cookie and Jan in New York

Sunbeams from the stained glass windows shined into the Cathedral as we slowly walked past the beautiful carved statues of the saints. Lighting candles together, we knelt down and said a prayer at the statue of the Blessed Virgin. After buying some postcards, we strolled back to the limousine.

"Where are we going now?" asked Peggy.

"It's another surprise. You'll have to wait and see." The limousine headed for the New York Heliport on the East River. Peggy and Cookie were surprised and a little apprehensive at first. However, they put their fears behind and stepped into the helicopter. I sat in the front seat with the pilot, while Cookie and Peg sat in the rear. Holding hands tightly as the flying bird climbed into the sky, we admired the spectacular views of the East River. We flew as far as the George Washington Bridge and then reversed direction, as the pilot headed towards Rockefeller Center, another famous site in New York City.

"Would you like to see it closer?" the pilot asked.

Enthusiastically, I replied "Yes, that would be great!" He bravely flew down through the skyscrapers, practically landing on the ice rink where people from all over the world were skating.

"This is not my normal tour, but I want this trip to be unforgettable," the pilot remarked. This was a once-in-a-lifetime view of the famous site that Peggy, Cookie, and I had visited in the past, but not from this angle. Hovering over the rink for about fifteen seconds, he pulled us back up through the tall buildings and headed towards the downtown area.

Flying over the Stock Exchange and Trinity Church on his way to the Statue of Liberty was a fascinating sight. As we got closer to "The Lady," I could not help but notice that the top of her head was as well sculptured as the rest of her body. I was impressed, because at the time the Statue was being carved, there were no helicopters. The Frenchmen who gave Her as a gift to America had no idea that people would be gazing at her hairdo. She had perfect form from head to toe. A true work of art! Seeing the Statue with the Manhattan skyline in the background was sensational! Although the experience was unique, Peggy and Cookie were glad to get their feet back on solid ground.

We hopped back into our limousine and drove to a restaurant on the East River, where we enjoyed refreshments and reminisced about days gone by. After about a half hour, the time had arrived to bid each other farewell. Shedding a few tears as we parted, we hugged and returned to our three separate worlds. I wondered, *When would we see each other again?* Only God knew.

"The Sea Dream"

Traveling from Dallas to New York, then to Florida and Boise, Idaho in 1991 convincing people to join me in my quest to provide *dream* locations for *Dare to Dream* events was evidence to me of God's favor. It seemed that He was divinely directing me to speak to the right people, at the right place, and at the right time.

Divine Appointments

One such occasion was birthed after church on a Sunday afternoon in Ft. Lauderdale, Florida in 1991. As my sister, Peggy, and I enjoyed lunch at a restaurant on the Intra-coastal Waterway, enormous yachts cruised by with people living the lifestyle of the rich and famous. "Wouldn't it be fabulous to have a yacht as a classroom for the kids I visited at the shelter last week?" I asked Peggy.

She looked at me as though I was crazy, and replied, "Jan, you don't even know anyone with a rowboat; how do you expect to see yourself on a yacht?"

"I can picture it!" I answered with excitement. "Imagine a yacht filled with brokenhearted kids cruising down this fabulous waterway with people who really cared about them." Within five minutes after I spoke those words, a fifty-two-foot Bluewater Cruiser, "The Sea Dream," pulled directly next to the dock where we were sitting. I got up and walked towards the yacht. I shouted to the captain on the bridge, "I like the name of your boat."

He yelled back, "Thank you, and who are you?"

"I'm a lady from Dallas who creates classes in *dream* settings for disadvantaged youth," I answered reaching up and handing my business card to a member of the crew.

He passed it up to the captain who looked at my card and exclaimed, "*Dare to Dream*! Wow, what a coincidence."

I took a leap of faith and asked, "Captain, would you be willing to provide your yacht as a classroom for some youngsters from a local shelter?"

He waited a moment and then responded, "Jan, you have hit my hot button. I would be delighted."

I was thrilled with his answer and said, "I'm flying back to Dallas tomorrow and will call you as soon as I return to make definite arrangements." We exchanged phone numbers and parted company.

After returning to Dallas, I spoke with one of my Board members telling him that I needed some funds to fly back to

Ft. Lauderdale to create this special event. By God's grace, I got what I asked for and my dream became a reality.

Two weeks later, the Captain warmly greeted the smiling youngsters at the front door of his home in Ft. Lauderdale. Refreshments were served, and the teenagers were invited to take their seats in the chairs on the dock facing the water. After the captain and his crew gave them instructions on water safety, I shared some of my story. By the look in the eyes of the teens, I knew I had their respect. I told them that God considers each of them a rare and priceless treasure, and that, with His help, anything is possible.

After my talk, the teenagers were in great spirits as they enthusiastically boarded the "Sea Dream." Two girls danced on the deck of the yacht to the Latin tunes I played on my battery-operated keyboard. As we cruised by fabulous homes with swimming pools and jet boats, it appeared as though everyone was having a great time. However, all of a sudden one of the girls began weeping. I asked, "Sweetheart, is something wrong?"

She replied, "No, Miss Jan, I've never felt this happy before in my whole life." Later in the day, another girl revealed to me that she hated men. Realizing that she probably had legitimate reasons to feel that way, I asked, "What do you think of our captain who invited us to enjoy this cruise on his yacht?"

She answered, "Well, I've never met anyone like him before." I could tell that she wanted to talk with me, so I invited her downstairs to the galley. She told me one of the most horrible stories I had ever heard. Tears rolled down her face as she lowered her head and said, "Mom invited men into our home to have sex with me while she watched." My heart broke as I comforted and encouraged her to pray that she could one day forgive her mother and the men that hurt her. Cradling her in my arms, I kissed her forehead.

It is this kind of story that causes me to become more passionate about planting seeds of encouragement in the

DIVINE APPOINTMENTS

hearts of fragile youngsters who desperately need our love, prayers, and direction.

In December 1991, a Florida radio personality heard about our trip on "The Sea Dream" and telephoned me in Dallas for an interview. She listened to the history of *Dare to Dream* and why I was so intent on helping unfortunate children. When she invited me to participate in the *20th Annual Ft. Lauderdale Christmas Boat Parade*, I was elated. Within a few weeks I packed my bags and headed back to Florida.

Two days before the parade, I invited Kids Crusaders Against Child Abuse—an organization that helps foster kids and their families—to attend a *Dare to Dream* seminar at their headquarters in Sunrise, Florida. My goal was to explain to the foster parents how vitally important their role is in the lives of the children. After my talk, I surprised them and announced that the foster children would be invited to join me on "The Sea Dream" for the Christmas boat parade.

"Really? I can hardly believe it!" one of the staff cheered.

I emphasized to the foster parents and the children that this was not just another boat ride—it was the direct result of a dream and a prayer.

Two days later, on a gorgeous day in December, twenty excited foster children arrived at the Captain's home. I handed each of them a *Dare to Dream* T-shirt to wear on the cruise. "The Sea Dream" was decorated with multicolored Christmas lights, along with a large plastic Santa Claus figure attached to the vessel. The large *Dare to Dream* banner displayed on both sides of the yacht was an extra surprise for me! Being aware of the sad stories of the children, it warmed my heart to see them looking so happy while they lined up on the dock ready to board the yacht.

She Dares to *Dream*

Foster children waiting to board "The Sea Dream"

It was exciting to watch the different vessels lining up for the parade—fishing boats, catamarans, along with fabulous luxury cruisers. The most exciting entry was a large yacht towing a trampoline with circus performers on it. Comedian Joan Rivers was on a vessel directly behind us. The teenagers couldn't resist waving and yelling, "We love you, Joan."

Nothing was left undone—delicious food and refreshments provided by a women's club, the sounds of Christmas carols being sung by our overjoyed youngsters echoing across the water, and the unusually calm seas as we floated through the water. Waving spectators clapped their hands as we cruised by. As the sun was setting, a rainbow of colors reflected on the water from the Christmas lights on the yachts and the extraordinary decorations from the homes on the shore. I had to pinch myself to make sure that I wasn't dreaming.

A Room at the Top

In April 1991, I was invited along with a group of women to voice our concerns in Austin, Texas, with our Congressmen. At one of the gatherings, I met a lady who worked with the Texas Youth Commission. After chatting awhile, I told her about *Dare to Dream* and said that I would be delighted to give a presentation to TYC youth during my visit, either at their facility or at a *dream* location if I could find one. She was excited about the idea, so we exchanged phone numbers.

The next day, I searched all over the city trying to find just the right location for a presentation, but nothing seemed to work. The luxurious hotels were booked, the red paddle wheeler needed work, and the circular boardroom at the hotel wasn't available. Then, after lunch, something wonderful happened. Walking down Congress Avenue toward the Capitol building, I spotted an extraordinary tall pink building with a top that looked like a cathedral.

I said to my friend, "Let's go inside."

"For what?" she asked.

I explained, "I feel strongly that we should just go inside." Entering the two-story, marble-floored, lobby, we headed for the elevators. Pushing the top button, we got off at the penthouse. I walked to the receptionist's desk and introduced myself.

"Do you have any board rooms on this floor?"

She replied, "Yes, that's all we have at this level."

I was thrilled, and asked, "Do you have a board room facing the Capitol building?"

She smiled and said, "Come with me." Wondering where she was taking us, we walked down to the end of a long narrow hallway. She opened the door to an amazing three-sided glass boardroom with high ceilings that faced the Capitol.

"What a view. This is perfect!"

"Perfect for what?" she asked.

"I'd like to invite some boys from the Texas Youth Commission up here for a special *Dare to Dream* program."

With a frown on her face she asked, "Are you talking about juvenile delinquents?"

"Oh no, I'm talking about young men who have made some mistakes but can change with a little help from people like you and me." She was silent for a moment.

Then I asked, "Would you be willing to reserve this room for a presentation this evening?"

"This evening? I'm sorry, but the person who makes those decisions is out of town."

I promptly asked, "Well, does that mean he left you in charge?"

She thought a moment and with confidence replied, "Well, yes, I guess I am." Jumping ahead, I started describing how I wanted the room set up, when she interrupted me.

"There's only one problem; the building will be locked at 7:00 p.m."

I immediately blurted out, "I'd like to talk with the security guard in charge and see if he would be willing to stay longer." She looked at me like that was impossible. Nevertheless, I convinced the guard, and our request was granted!

At 7:00 p.m. sharp, the guard winked at me as thirty-two robust looking young men between the ages of fifteen and twenty and the staff from the Texas Youth Commission walked into the lobby. After greeting the group at the front door, I escorted them into the elevator. Entering with wide-eyes, one of the boys enthusiastically pushed the top button. For some, this was their first elevator ride.

At the top, I guided them down the narrow hallway towards the boardroom and opened the door to the *dream* location. Cool rap music played on the boom box as they entered the room. The boys had a surprised look on their faces as they gravitated towards the enormous floor-to-ceiling windows looking out at the city with its landscape of giant architecture. A young man I had met in a restaurant the week before strummed his guitar, while the teenagers and guests got acquainted with one another. The boys appeared as though they were enjoying themselves as they devoured some delicious sandwiches provided by the lady in

DIVINE APPOINTMENTS

charge. This woman, who obviously had a change of heart from when we first met, invited everyone to take their seats and then introduced me.

The stories I told the youth provided a platform for us to quickly connect. As I was speaking, the sun had disappeared behind the large buildings, the lights of the city came on, the Capitol dome was illuminated, and the view of the city of Austin was spectacular!

Jan giving a presentation to Texas Youth Commission teens in Austin, Texas 1991

In my final statements I told the audience, "You can live life with the lights on or the lights off; it's a personal choice." I told the boys how God clearly led me to this amazing team of people who helped orchestrate this *dream* event within a single day! The security guard graciously stayed after hours to let us in; the lady in charge, not only provided the room, but also asked women from the community to provide sandwiches and punch; and the guitarist was willing to take his precious time to provide music for us. The boys and the staff of the Texas Youth Commission were in awe as they became aware of God's hand in action that day.

♥ *"Ask, and it will be given to you; seek, and you will find; knock, and it will be opened to you. For everyone who asks receives, and he who seeks finds, and to him who knocks it will be opened"*
(Matthew 7: 7-8).

Music on the Mountain

That same year, my former landlord and friend, Betty Baker, invited me to visit her in Boise, Idaho. Assuring her that I would love to come, I told her that one of my goals while in her hometown would be to create some *Dare to Dream* events for youth.

"Betty, I would need to borrow your telephone and your car for one day."

She replied, "Great! Come on!"

When I arrived, she warmly greeted me and asked, "Since you don't know anyone here, how do you expect to make your contacts?"

With assurance, I told her, "I'll search through the telephone book and find children's homes and people who will help me." In her humorous way, she commented, "Go for it, Jan."

The next day, I visited the Emancipation Home for boys in downtown Boise. The Director was intrigued with my story. "If I could find a special place to conduct a *dream* event for the boys, would you be willing to let them come out of the shelter?" I asked.

With disbelief, he remarked, "Jan, nobody ever asked that question. Yes, I'd love for our boys to join you." I told him I had no idea where this event would take place, but that I would call him as soon as I discovered a location. I wondered, *Where would I want to go and what would I like to do if I was a teenager in a group home?*

It didn't take long for me to decide that skiing would be on the top of my list. I drove to Bogus Mountain and spoke with the management, asking them to partner with me to create this event for the boys. In preparation for this trip, I requested a personal tour of the slopes. I also asked for skis, boots, poles, and ski lessons for the boys. My last request was to have a private area reserved on the top of the mountain where we could have lunch and I could give a presentation to the teens. God's favor was with me, and all of my requests were granted!

DIVINE APPOINTMENTS

The director of the boys' home was amazed when I told him my plans. He said, "The boys wanted to go skiing for quite some time, but we just didn't have the money."

The next day, the boys, along with a staff member, boarded a van and headed to the slopes. Excitement was high as they were fitted for skis and boots for the first time in their lives. During their lesson, they discovered that skiing didn't come naturally.

Dare to Dream, Bogus Mountain in Boise, Idaho

Sitting on the chairlift two-by-two and holding my keyboard on my lap, we slowly climbed the majestic snow-covered mountain. Our reserved area on the side of the lodge was waiting and the boys went directly to the chow line. Enjoying a delicious lunch and a spectacular view of the mountain range, I proceeded to give a short presentation encouraging the teens to become role models for boys just like themselves. When I finished, one of the teens volunteered to sing and play the keyboard. He was thrilled for the opportunity to entertain his peers on the mountaintop. He said, "I feel like I'm in a dream, Miss Jan."

After my talk, some of the boys, with a staff member, skied down the novice slopes. At the end of the day, we got back into the van and returned to the boys' home, exhausted. We hugged, wished each other well, and parted company.

A few weeks later, I received this letter from the director of the boys home dated March 14, 1991.

Dearest Jan:

Please accept our warmest thanks from the staff and kids for your efforts on our behalf. I'm in awe of your ability to put together a wonderful adventure for the kids in a few days as it usually takes weeks of planning and knocking on doors. You have left an indelible print on the hearts of the kids. Not only had they recently asked to go skiing (we couldn't go because of lack of funds), but they were truly impacted by your words of encouragement and hope. Every youth caring agency needs visiting angels like you to come around once in a while! Jan, we need people like you to keep us on our toes.

With you, serving others,
Facility Director

♥ *"Now to Him who is able to do exceedingly abundantly above all that we ask or think, according to the power that works in us, to Him be glory in the church by Christ Jesus to all generations, forever and ever"* (Ephesians 3:20-21).

Released from the Chains

On that same trip to Idaho, I was introduced to a place called the Pratt Boy's Ranch—a facility for incarcerated youth. I telephoned the ranch and introduced myself to the director. I told him what the mission was about and that I would like to visit and speak to their boys.

He remarked, "Nobody ever wants to come up to see these guys. They're tough, crude, and have been in a lot of trouble. Besides, we're two hours away from Boise. But, if you really want to come, I'll send a car to pick you up."

"Great, I'll be waiting for you."

A staff member drove over an hour to meet me. We slowly began our long journey up the mountain to the ranch. Once we arrived, the director introduced himself and had another staff member drive me further up the dusty mountain in his red pickup truck. When we approached the boys, I was startled when I saw them chained together working with shovels and picks.

I asked, "Would you be willing to release the boys from those chains and allow them to come down the mountain to have lunch with me?" Surprised that I wanted to spend my time with these tough teens, he agreed to my request.

I told him, "Whatever rotten things these boys have done, they're still God's children and need encouragement to change their lives." Their chains were removed, and the boys hopped into the pickup trucks and traveled down the mountain to the main house. After cleaning up, these bad boys each politely introduced themselves and thanked me for coming.

"The situation you are in right now is temporary. I want you to know that God loves you and will help you change your way of living if you'll let Him into your life. Start reading the Bible; it's an anchor through the storms. He can restore you from all the broken pieces of your life." The look in their eyes changed from hardness to tenderness as I planted seeds of love and encouragement. With tears in their eyes, they hugged me like a bunch of little kids saying good-bye to a Mom they might never see again.

♥ *"My purpose is that they may be encouraged in heart and united in love, so that they may have the full richness of complete understanding, in order that they may know the mystery of God, namely Christ, in whom are hidden all the treasures of wisdom and knowledge"*
(Colossians 2:2-3 NIV).

Ladies Choice

On that same trip, besides taking the boys from the Emancipation Home skiing and visiting the Pratt Boys Ranch, I also visited the Syringa Girls Home, housing youngsters between the ages of ten and seventeen. Some were runaways who had been neglected and abused, and some were in the foster care system waiting for another placement. The director introduced me to the residents, and after hearing my story, they related to me and asked me to join them for dinner. Enjoying a meal together at a large banquet table in the dining room, I asked if they'd like to share their dreams. At first, no one spoke, and then slowly they finally opened up:

"My dream is to go home when my mom gets out of jail."

"I want a family that will love me."

"I want to be a social worker to help kids like us."

"I want to be a police officer."

"I wish my dad would stop drinking."

"I just want a family."

After dinner, some of the girls asked me if I'd like to see their bedrooms. Taking my hand, acting like little children skipping down the hallway, I entered one small room with a bed, an end table, and a small dresser. The rooms were clean and neat with colorful bedspreads and pretty café curtains on the windows. The girls wanted to show me what was their *home*, for now. They showed me pictures of friends and their few possessions. I wanted more time to visit with the girls, but it was getting late.

Before I left the home, I asked the director if I could invite the girls to join me for dinner at a restaurant one night.

The director answered, "Yes, that would be wonderful! Where will this take place?" I told her that I didn't know yet, but I'd let them know soon.

The manager of a restaurant, close to where I was staying, agreed to host the girls. Wanting to make the evening special, they reserved a separate area for our party and to top it off—the girls could order anything they wanted from the menu!

Arriving at the restaurant wearing their Sunday best, the fifteen girls walked in with their heads held high and smiles on their faces. They looked like one large happy family. One wouldn't have known that some of the girls had been raped, beaten, and many of them were abandoned and physically and verbally abused. Guiding them to our reserved area, they were seated, and the hostess handed them a menu telling them that they could order whatever they wanted.

The waiters and waitresses politely answered their numerous questions about the menu, how long they worked there, and even how much money they made. After the delicious dinner, including dessert, I took a group picture outside by the lake with a view of the snow-capped mountains in the background. The girls and the staff were grateful for our special evening and pleaded with me to return one day to visit them again.

That day arrived sooner than expected. I invited the girls to tour the State Capitol, where they had their photo taken outside on the steps, with the impressive Capitol Dome in the background.

Excited, one girl said, "Wow Jan, we've never been in the Capitol before!" I told them to get a good education and stay close to God. "Learn to enjoy reading and stay in school; perhaps one day you'll have a job in this very important building." Seeds were planted that day, and the girls were excited about *daring to dream*.

♥ *"The Lord will fulfill His purpose for me..."*
   (Psalm 138:8 NIV).

A Party with a Purpose

To celebrate my fifty-first birthday, I wanted the teenagers I had visited in Idaho that week to be my guests at another *dream* location. I discovered the Hoff Building—an eleven-story structure built in 1929. A circular glass top, added in 1979, offered a spectacular panoramic view of Boise and the nearby mountains. It was called the "Top of the Hoff," and was exactly what I was looking for—a penthouse overlooking the Capitol with a large banquet room one floor below.

The manager was fascinated as I told him about my experiences and how generous the community had been in providing *dream* settings for the youngsters. I took this opportunity and asked, "Would you consider donating a banquet room for my birthday party with some sandwiches and punch for the youth?"

He graciously agreed and said, "Yes, it would be an honor to help you and the kids."

A few days later, the groups of youngsters I had visited the previous week jammed into the elevator and arrived at the penthouse ballroom. Walking up one story to the top level, they peered out the windows at the fabulous view of Boise and the State Capitol. A little while later, one by one, they paraded back downstairs to the banquet room. It was filled with round tables, flowers, and china plates and silverware, looking like it had been prepared for the academy awards. The youth enjoyed delicious sandwiches and punch as I gave a *Dare to Dream* presentation.

"God has a special plan for each one of you. Stay away from alcohol and drugs and from people who smoke like a chimney or drink like a fish. These things will rub off on you if you're not careful." I challenged them to stay in school, get an education, and hang around people who loved God and country.

After my talk, the girls from the Syringa Home came up to the podium with a surprise. They presented me with a large banner, signed by each of them, which said, "Happy Birthday, Jan. We love you and thank you!" During their presentation, a fifteen-year-old girl handed me a note that read,

> *I was alone and afraid in a world I never made. I closed my eyes and dared to dream. I dreamed of a world of laughter and bright smiling faces. When I opened my eyes, all I could see were sad and hardened faces. It was then that I realized, those are the faces of laughter with just a little help.*

DIVINE APPOINTMENTS

What a birthday! The room was filed with youth from the Emancipation Home, the Syringa Girls Home, and the Pratt Boys Ranch. It was the best birthday present I could have had. I was humbled and grateful for the Lord's guidance for this *party with a purpose.*

♥ *"You will show me the path of life; in your presence is fullness of joy; at your right hand are pleasures forevermore"*
(Psalm 16:11).

Flying High

While driving towards the airport in Addison, Texas, I discovered an airline hanger with the words "Million-Air" written on the front. Intrigued with the name, I parked my car, walked inside and asked the receptionist if I could speak to the director of operations. The impressive lobby with its tall windows overlooking the runway was filled with large leather couches and glass tables. I thought, *What a great place to conduct Dare to Dream classes.*

After meeting the director and telling him about *Dare to Dream*, he agreed to host our classes at their facility. A few weeks after my visit, I invited two *Dare to Dream* volunteers to tour the Million-Air facility. To my surprise, five Red Baron pilots, dressed in flight suits with red scarves draped around their necks, were having coffee and relaxing in the pilot's lounge.

I asked, "What are you men up to?"

One pilot answered, "We're supposed to be giving rides to raise funds for a charity, but no one is showing up."

Jan ready to take flight in Addison, Texas

I promptly remarked, "I'm here."

"Would you like to go up?" he asked.

I answered "Absolutely!"

Walking out to the runway, we saw two open cockpit two-seater airplanes. Wearing my blue dress and Million-Air flight jacket, I struggled getting up on the wing, where the pilot politely helped me climb into the back seat. Once seated and buckled up, I looked to the left and watched my volunteer get into the plane next to me. It was thrilling as both planes traveled down the runway and ascended into the sky, side by side.

Jan and Red Baron Pilot—Addison Airtort

The twists and turns made me feel like I was on a living roller coaster. I felt really brave as we zoomed over Addison airport, flying upside down without falling out of the plane.

Would I do it again? Definitely!

Two weeks later, youngsters from local shelters and youth homes entered the Million-Air hanger with heads spinning, admiring the luxurious facility. Listening to every word the staff person had to say, they toured the pilot's lounge, which housed a Jacuzzi, a pool table, and a large TV. On a number of occasions, we held *Dare to Dream* classes inside one of the aircraft. Other times we used the boardroom upstairs. The youth and volunteers enjoyed lunch while a staff person shared information about the facility and the variety of jobs available at Million-Air. The boys and girls had the opportunity to ask questions and thoroughly enjoyed the session.

Later, I passed out blank business cards and asked them to dream of a job they would love to have. "Stretch out of your comfort zone and don't let your past, your lack of education, finances, or family influence what you write." I asked them to close their eyes and *dream,* as I played a medley of tunes on my battery-operated keyboard.

As they opened their eyes, I instructed the group to write down their names, their titles, and the name of the company of their dreams. Some of the youngsters wrote counselor, welder, teacher, rap artist, and singer. Some shared their dreams verbally, while others had difficulty dreaming. I encouraged them to pray and ask for God's purpose and direction for their lives.

"The Best Years of Your Life" Contest

As I mentioned before, creating an event at the White House was one of my life's goals. To prepare the way, I traveled to Washington to search for a group home with youngsters who could one day be my guests at the *dream* event. I asked some civic clubs, "Are there any group homes for destitute kids here in Washington?" Over and over I was told, "We don't have places like that here." I found that hard to believe, so I opened the phone book and discovered exactly what I was looking for— "The Sasha Bruce House," a home for troubled youth right there in Washington D.C.

After visiting the director and telling him about *Dare to Dream,* he was amazed that I would take the time and expense to come so far to encourage his youngsters. After telling him about my White House dream, he remarked, "I'll look forward to hearing from you someday!"

I left that day wondering, *How on earth will something like this ever happen?*

A few years later, a friend read an article in a magazine about the The National Tour Association putting on a "Best Years of Your Life" contest. She encouraged me to enter and tell them about my work with children. I hesitated at first, but then decided to write a letter. A month later, I received a letter in the mail informing me that I was one of the four National winners! The winner would recieve two round-trip tickets to anywhere USAir traveled. Since I was extremely busy with the operations of *Dare to Dream*, I asked if they would extend the deadline for another six months. They said that wasn't possible.

Since I had to take the trip before the year was over, I prayed asking God to help me know if this was the right time to proceed with my White House dream. I clearly felt that if USAir had only *one* direct flight from Dallas to Washington, D.C. *that* would be my signal to go ahead. As fate would have it—there was only *one* direct flight to Washington! I knew this was the time, and now I had to put a plan into action. It was already October, and the December 31st deadline was right around the corner.

Picking up the phone, I called Texas Congressman, Sam Johnson, a man I respected. I told him I had won "The Best Years of Your Life" contest, and that my dream was to create a special event in the White House.

It was music to my ears when he said, "Congratulations, Jan. I will get my people right on it and let you know if the White House is available."

A few days later, he called back and told me, "The White House is totally booked with Christmas festivities, but I'll check on the next best thing—the Capitol!" Within a short time, he phoned back and said, "The Capitol is available, and if you agree, we'll book a special room for you." He sounded as excited as I was!

I wondered, *Where will I stay, and how will I pay for all of this?* Opening the directory I had kept from my days with the National

Divine Appointments

Speakers Association, I found that the CEO of the Marriott Hotel chain was located in Virginia. I made the call and spoke directly to him. He asked me to fax the letter about winning the contest to him, and within one hour, my phone rang.

His secretary told me, "You have two rooms for one week at the Marriott Hotel on Pennsylvania Avenue, two blocks from the White House." I was ecstatic. A *Dare to Dream* volunteer, Susan, who was also a wonderful singer, agreed to accompany me and to assist me on the trip.

Jan with Congressman Sam Johnson

Arriving at the snow-covered Dulles International airport, we were so excited that we could hardly wait to hop in a cab and get to our hotel. Once I arrived at my room, there was a message from Congressman Johnson inviting me to join him the next day for breakfast at the Capitol Hill Club.

We met at his office, and I showed the Congressman a video from a Channel 11 news spot in Dallas featuring *Dare to Dream*. Next on the agenda was breakfast at the Capitol Hill Club. As we entered the main room, I was mesmerized as I scanned the walls filled with enormous life-sized paintings of our Presidents and their wives. Being a patriotic person, visiting with Congressman Sam Johnson was a real honor for me. Twenty-nine years earlier, after serving in the U.S. Air Force as a highly decorated fighter pilot, Congressman Johnson returned home to Texas. He flew combat missions in both the Korean and Vietnam Wars and was a Prisoner of War in Hanoi for nearly seven years.

"Jan, I'm glad I can help you. My staff will put a schedule together for your week here in Washington, and I believe you'll have a terrific visit."

Once I knew the event was going to happen in the Capitol, I called the director of the Sasha Bruce House.

He exclaimed, "You're back! I'm so pleased."

I told him, "With the help of Congressman Johnson, I'd like you and your residents to be my guests in a private room at the United States Capitol building for a *Dare to Dream* presentation."

He gasped, "Really? How terrific for our kids." He invited me to join them for dinner that evening.

When I arrived, I was greeted by the staff and was directed to my seat at the long dining table along with sixteen teenagers. Getting acquainted over dinner was quite an experience. They asked me to tell them about my life and why I came from Dallas to visit them in Washington D.C.

After dinner, I shared a little about my background. Then, a few of the teens shared their tragic stories of abandonment and rejection. Some of the teens were from the streets, and were trying to get off drugs. People they trusted had abused many of them.

Over dessert, I shared some of my dreams for the future. I passed out some paper and encouraged them to write down their dreams. Some wrote a note, but others wrote nothing. Three of the youth wrote:

"I want a family to adopt me."

"I want to go home, but my mom is in jail."

"I want people to stop hitting one another."

I told them that we can't change yesterday, but with a good attitude and a good education things will get better. I then revealed that in a few days, they were going to be my guests for a *Dare to Dream* event in the Nation's Capitol. Their eyes lit up like candles in the night.

Honoring the great State of Texas by wearing a tan-fringed vest, blue jeans, boots, and a cowboy hat, I invited two servicemen in uniform who were visiting the Capitol to join our presentation. I prayed that I would be able to articulate with passion my love of God and country. The American flag, my keyboard, the chairs, and the lectern with the Presidential Seal were all in place.

"Welcome! I'm delighted that you are here with me today. Because men and women fought and died so that we could have the right to speak, let us stand and honor them by reciting the Pledge of Allegiance to the Flag." Some of the youth put their hand over their hearts and recited the pledge. A few did not know the words.

Jan speaking in the Capitol Building, Washington D.C.

"We live in a great country that allows us to receive an education and opportunities to work and live a good life. We have freedom of speech and of religion. Our possibilities for the future are endless. If we stay off drugs, develop a good attitude, and surround ourselves with good role models, we can achieve our dreams. Knowledge is power, and with prayer and commitment, we can change our world."

Without knowing that Christmas is my favorite holiday, a member of Congressman Johnson's staff told me, "Jan, we have some surprises for you. You will be attending the lighting of the Capitol Christmas tree, and will have an escorted tour of the White House for you and twenty-five of your guests."

Once I caught my breath, she informed me, "We'd also like you and two guests to attend the lighting of the White House Christmas tree."

My head was spinning; this was much more than I ever expected.

The next evening, the weather was cold and brisk as chairs were being placed in rows on the lawn of the Capitol building. The Christmas tree stood majestically waiting for that special moment when the lights would be lit and its colors would glisten against the snow. Dignitaries gathered as the festivities were about to begin. Susan and I took our seats as the military band's music rang out playing "God Bless America." Tears flowed down my cheeks as I thought, *What an honor for me to sit elbow to elbow with dignified men and women who are serving our country with such pride.* The magical moment arrived—the switch for the multi-colored lights lit up the tree and the Capitol dome also became lit. The applause of the crowd echoed from the hill on which we sat. It was a marvelous evening that I will never forget.

The next day, I picked up the phone and dialed the Director of the Sasha Bruce House and said, "Hello, this is Jan Tennyson, the lady from Dallas who invited you to the event at the Capitol. In two days from now, I'd like you and the same youngsters to join me for a private tour of the White House."

He was overjoyed and could hardly believe that his youngsters were really going to the White House! Standing outside the main gate, I called on the private White House security telephone to announce that our group had arrived. Secret service men escorted us directly inside. Walking past the forty-eight beautifully decorated Christmas trees in the grand hall was absolutely amazing. Strolling leisurely from room to room admiring the colorful walls, high ceilings, fabulous furniture and incredible paintings, was an experience that would not be soon forgotten. The delight on the faces of the youth and staff made all our efforts worthwhile. This was genuinely a true *Dare to Dream* Christmas.

Susan and I were about to experience another great night in Washington D.C. We were invited to view the lighting of the Christmas tree across from the White House lawn! In spite of the pouring down rain, excitement was high as we were escorted to our reserved seats. Listening to the patriotic music made me feel like I was seated in one of the finest theatres in the world. Flags waved, as celebrities sat on the stage with umbrellas in hand. The military band protected the tuba and other instruments with clear plastic coverings as they entertained the crowd. Lee Greenwood sang "God Bless the USA" and the television and movie star, Lucy Arnez, also entertained the crowd.

President George Bush, Sr. gave a special message:

"Barbara and I want to dedicate this Christmas tree to the children of America, for they are more than our future; they are our present." He reminded us that we must love one another in order to achieve peace. "Our prayers are with our military and the ones they cherish ... May I simply say, let us think of the children of Somalia, too, the children everywhere who live in fear and want. Our prayers are with them, and may their families be safe and the sporadic fighting over there end soon."

After his short talk, the President gave the signal—"Barbara, let's light the tree."

The crowd stood and gave a roaring applause. The gigantic tree with hundreds of multi-colored lights glistened in all its majesty as the festivities were coming to a close. I found it interesting to find out that each year, a magnificent tree is selected from a different State to stand on this strategic ground. Smaller Christmas trees decorated with ornaments created by children throughout the United State surrounded the main tree. I thought, *What a great symbol of unity*. How special to have your child's ornament displayed at the White House celebration.

These words are not just about winning "The Best Years of Your Life" contest; they are about what the Lord created in Washington D.C. *because* of winning the contest. I returned to Dallas with a grateful heart for the incredible opportunity to truly celebrate one of the best years of my life!

♥ *"...No eye has seen, no ear has heard, no mind has conceived what God has prepared for those who love him"*
(1 Corinthians 2:9 NIV).

PART THREE

A Spiritual Journey

My Happy Place

*"…But you are a chosen generation, a royal priesthood, a holy nation,
His own special people, that you may proclaim the praises of Him
who called you out of darkness into His marvelous light"*
(I Peter 2:9).

INTRODUCTION

This section is an honor for me to write because it's not about me. It's about the call on my life influenced by the power of the Holy Spirit. It has taken me a lifetime to learn about a submitted and obedient heart. But once I stepped out and answered the call of God, He moved in ways more grand than I could ever have imagined.

I grew up in the Roman Catholic Church, received my first Holy Communion when I was six, and the sacrament of Confirmation at the age of thirteen. Going to Confession on Saturdays and receiving Holy Communion at Sunday Mass was a weekly ritual. However, being devoted to religion with no idea about a personal relationship with Christ left me spiritually bankrupt.

Coming from a strict foster home, my life was very controlled. Consequently, as a young adult, I wanted to spread my wings and explore new horizons. Staying out late drinking cocktails and dancing in clubs was what normal young people did—or so I thought. Some friends smoked cigarettes to look cool, but it was not for me. Making out (kissing) with my boyfriend was an accepted activity, but, when emotions raged, my conscience wouldn't allow me to follow through on my feelings.

Knowing the right thing to do and what not to do kept me a virgin into my twenties. However, because I was young and foolish, I had a horrible experience while on a vacation in the

Bahamas. A casual acquaintance, whom I trusted, attacked me. I was twenty-two. My girlhood dream of being pure for the man I would marry was shattered, and I regret to this day that I was too scared, too embarrassed, and not emotionally strong enough to report the vicious attack to the police. Humiliated and broken, not knowing how to hold my head up high extended my years of low self-esteem. Fear of anyone finding out caused me to live a life filled with intimidation.

I did not plan my spiritual journey, God did. He took me into His arms and held me when I didn't deserve it, or even know that He was there.

May these stories of His love and direction inspire you to know that regardless of the circumstances that come your way, God will never leave you nor forsake you. He will be with you always.

Chapter Eleven

My Transformation

A Mission Field in the Making

As a child, unlike some of the children in my class at school, I *wanted* to go to church. The fact that I could not understand a word spoken at the Latin Mass didn't matter. I liked the warm atmosphere and the peaceful feeling I felt inside.

In Catholic school, the Sisters of Mercy taught me to be kind, to tell the truth, and to go to confession when I had committed a sin. They must have inspired me, because when I was seventeen, I thought of becoming a Maryknoll nun. I loved the fact that these Sisters traveled to faraway places and helped children. Intrigued with their commitment to service, I wrote to find out more information.

I learned that the Maryknoll Order was founded in 1912 in Maryknoll, New York. They were the first group of Catholic nuns in the United States to devote their lives in service overseas. Their modern day literature reads: "Maryknoll Sisters are committed to crossing boundaries, whether cultural, social, religious, geographic, or economic to proclaim the Good News of the Reign of God."

After reading the requirements, which included remaining a single Catholic woman living in a convent and being willing to devote my life totally to God, I decided, *This was not the life for me.* After all, I was a young woman who wanted to have fun, dance and travel. God had a call on my life to reach out to children in need, but it was not as a Maryknoll nun.

A Turning Point

In 1988, as I was driving out of a parking lot in Dallas, I noticed Mamie McCullough, a speaker and author, waving to get my attention. When I drove my car close to her, she remarked, "Jan, I'd like you to hear Jerry Johnston speak. He is one of the finest youth evangelists in the country. He'll be speaking this Wednesday night right across the street at Prestonwood Church."

Never having set foot inside a Baptist Church before, I was a little apprehensive. However, I accepted Mamie's suggestion and decided to attend. Friendly people greeted me as I entered the building and guided me to the largest sanctuary I had ever seen. Watching smiling young people carrying Bibles and young men wearing tailored pants and dress shoes on a weeknight was unfamiliar to me. I sat on the back row and promised myself that I would listen to the speaker, and then dart out as soon as he finished his sermon.

The sanctuary was packed, and the spontaneous standing ovation as Jerry Johnston came out on the stage startled me. He was young, tall, and good-looking.

"I grew up in a good family with a beautiful home, a good education, and a nice car. But, despite all my material wealth, I felt totally empty inside. Something was missing from my life." His discouragement and depression caused him to turn to drugs, alcohol, and women.

"I was headed on a downward spiral to a place called nowhere, and I wanted to end my life." One night after drinking and drugging—feeling totally despondent—he miraculously arrived safely at his apartment. Falling to his knees in his bedroom, he pleaded, "God, if you are real, I need your help. I can't go on this way anymore. I just want to die." That evening, something wonderful happened. Jesus came into his heart, and from that moment on, he never drank alcohol, nor did he use drugs ever again.

I was astounded by his story and totally engrossed as he looked out at the audience and said, "Now that you've heard what God did for me, I want to ask you two questions: If you know for sure that if you died tonight you would go to heaven, please stand up." People all over the auditorium stood to their feet; I wasn't one of them.

"To those of you who didn't stand, you may not be sure that you would go to heaven if you died tonight, but you really want to. Please stand if that is you." Of course I wanted to go to heaven, but I just wasn't sure that I'd make it.

"Those of you who want Christ in your heart, please come to the front of the auditorium and let me lead you in a prayer that will give you the assurance of eternity in heaven." I didn't budge. There was no way I was going to walk from the last row of that enormous sanctuary to the front of the church with everyone watching. Besides, everyone would think I was a sinner. Glued to my seat with my arms folded, I had an unusual feeling similar to butterflies fluttering in my stomach. Then suddenly, without any effort on my part, I found myself parading down the longest aisle I had ever seen. It was as if a shovel had picked me up and carried my body to the front of the church. I wasn't walking down on my own power and couldn't understand why tears were streaming down my face. Nothing like this had ever happened before.

Jerry then invited the people standing before him to bow their heads and repeat this prayer: "Lord, I know I'm a sinner.

I believe You died on the cross for me, and You rose from the dead. I'm sorry for anything I have done to offend You. Come into my heart and be my Lord and Savior. Teach me how to live and how to be the person you want me to be. Thank You for loving me. Amen."

The Bible says: *"If you confess with your mouth the Lord Jesus and believe in your heart that God has raised Him from the dead, you will be saved"* (Romans 10:9).

I loved God and I had religion; but until that evening, I didn't have a personal relationship with Jesus. Little did I know that this was the day I would have an encounter with God and would be born again. After that experience, my desires, my talk, and how I spent my time changed. I learned that only Jesus could help me, heal me, and make me whole.

> ♥ *"...Most assuredly, I say to you, unless one is born again, he cannot see the kingdom of God"*
> (John 3:3).

The invitation prayer is available to you and the promise of everlasting life can be yours. If you have not asked Jesus into your heart, you can do it right now. Pray the prayer, and reserve your place in heaven. He will do for you what He did for me.

A Breaking Point

March 1988 was the most stressful time of my life. Even though I had recently invited Christ into my heart, I was dating a man that I truly cared about, but was not living a holy life. Wanting God's best, I prayed, "Lord, if this is not the person you want me to spend the rest of my life with, remove him from me."

Before long, God did exactly that. We never had an argument, but little by little this man pulled away from my life. It devastated me. Unexpectedly that Christmas, he stopped by my home and handed me two round-trip tickets to Paris that he had won in a golf tournament. Without any questions, I took them and simply said, "Thank you." We never dated again. The following September, I invited my son, James, to join me on the trip. Years later, I found this note that I wrote one night in a folder:

> *With pink roses on my table, lovers walking hand in hand, and the romantic French language buzzing all around me, restaurateurs were folding their tablecloths closing up for the night. My pen begins to attack the paper writing down my confused feelings. Hate—very unlike me; Love—but my heart was broken; Fantasy—you sit across from me smiling; Resentment—you're not with me; and Fear—will I ever see you again?*
>
> *Conducting this conversation by pen is an interesting experience. It allows me to write, speak, feel love, and be angry without interruption. As I heal from my wounds, perhaps one day I'll remember this moment, smelling the fragrance of the roses and noticing the shadows in the cool night air. I suddenly realize that God and I will make it together. I will survive. But, comprehending how one can drop such passionate feelings of love in such a short time...for another, put me off balance. How could you marry someone else, so soon, on my birthday? I'm angry, sad, hurt, and thankful that you were taken from me. Not my choice, God's choice.*

Remembering yesterday's heartaches helps me realize how desperately I need to spend time reading the Bible to embrace peace and direction for my life. That same month, two of my miniature dachshunds died within one week. James moved from my home into his father's house. Lisa, not knowing for sure that she was choosing the right career, withdrew from college and also moved in with her dad. Dealing with an empty nest and feeling unappreciated, lonely, and worthless to my family made me think, *I was there for the tough times, but now that they are grown, they don't need me anymore.*

Despondent with my life, I started looking for love in all the wrong places and getting involved with people who didn't know God. Following in their footsteps, I stopped going to church and was miserable. Floods of hardships were pounding down on me, and I was losing my grip on life. Then, through it all, the Lord whispered—

> ♥ *"Come to me, all you who labor and are heavy laden, and I will give you rest. Take My yoke upon you, and learn from Me, for I am gentle and lowly in heart and you will find rest for your soul"*
> (Matthew 11:28-29).

In the mid 70s, Mary Crowley, founder of Home Interiors & Gifts, Inc., attended a performance of the Richardson Chorale Club when I was their choreographer. That day, we became acquainted and she told me, "Jan, I see something special in you. Make sure you follow your dream."

In 1988, after inviting Jesus into my heart, I was still a baby Christian attending Prestonwood Baptist church. I joined a Bible study in a private home. This was the open door for me to learn about the principles and promises of God. But, when each person prayed prayer requests verbally, I was uncomfortable. When my turn came, I simply said, "I pass." I could speak to God in my heart, but didn't know how to speak the words. During my morning walks, I forced myself to pray verbally, and found that speaking the name of Jesus was uncomfortable for me. Most people I knew spoke His name only when they were cursing. One day a friend told me, "Jan, make believe you are talking to your best friend. You can do it."

At another Bible study, someone asked me, "Jan, we know you grew up in foster care, but who adopted you?"

"I was never adopted; I lived in foster care my entire childhood."

The Bible teacher abruptly corrected me. "Jan, you were adopted by your heavenly Father a long time ago. He will never leave you nor forsake you." Glad tears wet my cheeks, and for the first time, I realized that I was accepted in the beloved and had a heavenly Father who truly loved me.

I continued church hopping, not knowing what I was searching for. On Sundays I would ask God, "Where do you want me to go to church today?" I visited various places and started meeting people who were committed Christians.

In 1990, on two occasions, I was invited to Hillcrest Church, an inter-denominational Bible church in North Dallas. Each time I visited, I wondered, *Who are those people standing at the altar rail praying for people? Why are they raising their hands when they sing? And what is everyone so happy about?*

Walking out of the church one day I wondered, *Just what kind of a church is this?* Regardless of my questions, I found myself attending their services and loving the people.

An Earth Angel Bouquet

My bouquet is overflowing with memories of people who planted the seeds of God's Word into my life and helped me grow spiritually. I could never mention all of them, but they know the impact they have made because I've told them. In this section, you will read about a few precious people who helped my wobbly legs become spiritually strong and who brought beauty and fragrance into my life:

One lady who attended Hillcrest Church said, "Jan, my husband and I normally sit in the same spot every Sunday and no matter what time you get here, I'll have this 'Reserved' sign on your seat. You can come and sit with us anytime."

Sitting next to June Bicking and her husband touched my heart and my life.

A few months later, I decided to branch out and sit on the opposite side of the church. When the pastor gave an invitation to pray at the prayer rail, I slowly walked up and knelt down. A tender lady took my hand as I said, "My family members are so wounded; I don't know how to pick up the broken pieces." Tears streamed down my face as she prayed for me. Once I returned to my seat, the Pastor, Dr. Morris Sheats, who is responsible for much of my spiritual growth, asked the people to introduce themselves to one another. My face was a mess and I didn't want to talk with anyone. However, God placed a beautiful lady right next to me. Her eyes sparkled like diamonds and she had one of the most beautiful smiles I had ever seen. She saw my tears, hugged me and said, "Do you have any idea how much Jesus loves you?" I felt an instant warmth that I had never experienced before surge through my body from head to toe.

On another occasion, that same woman asked, "Do you belong to a church?" I told her that I wasn't interested in joining anything right now.

She didn't give up. "Jan, God wants you to have a church home, and He doesn't want you church hopping any more. He wants you to belong and wants to bless you more than you can imagine." I thought about what she said, and after several months, I attended the new members class. By the final session, I knew I had found my church home. God used my new friend, Tansye Jackson, to brighten my garden and my outlook on life.

I soon became a member of Hillcrest Church and wanted to grow spiritually. I searched to find a class to attend before the Sunday service. Feeling like an anxious child on the first day of school, I walked up and down the hallway asking God

My Transformation

to show me where I belonged. Recognizing one of the teachers, I entered her classroom and sat down. I didn't have a clue what topic would be taught, but I felt comfortable because a lady that I had met before, Dorothy Moore, was the teacher.

The topic that day turned out to be *Spiritual Warfare*, which was totally unfamiliar territory for me. But I had promised God that whichever class He sent me to, I would be committed to attend every session. Discussions about demons and generational curses made me most uncomfortable. At the last session, Dorothy told the class, "Instead of teaching today, let us pray for one another, and Jan, I'd like to pray for you first." I was honored.

Powerful words were prayed over me, and I walked out of her class a totally different person. From that day forward, the gift and power of the Holy Spirit brought a depth of spirituality I had not known before. Dorothy Moore, founder of Reconciliation Outreach ministry in Dallas, Texas, was the fragrant flower who made a dynamic impact on my life.

Shortly after accepting Jesus into my heart, many Christians encouraged me to be water baptized. I thought, *Why is that necessary? I was baptized as a baby.* Almost two years passed before I finally realized that as an infant, I didn't choose to be baptized; my parents made that decision. Finally surrendering my will, I told God that I was willing to be water baptized when and where He directed me. I later thought, *Wouldn't it be incredible to be baptized in the River Jordan where Jesus was baptized?*

In 1989, Dorothy Moore and her husband, Bob, invited me to a Fourth of July party at their home on Cedar Creek Lake outside of Dallas. On this beautiful day, while sitting on a blanket on a hill overlooking the lake with one of the homeless men from the ministry, I asked, "Wouldn't this be a perfect place to have a baptism?" He agreed, and left to ask Sister Dorothy about having a baptism at the lake that day.

She said, "We can't have a baptism today, because the men's pastor, Robert Cook, isn't here." Discouraged, I thought, *Maybe*

I'm just not holy enough. Maybe I need to read the Bible more. At about 4:00 p.m. Pastor Robert Cook unexpectedly arrived at the gathering.

"If anyone wants to be water baptized, come to the boat dock," one of Dorothy's staff announced.

My heart leaped, and in an instant, I knew this was going to be my day. It was finally going to happen! Dorothy's husband, Bob, took my arm and guided me towards the lake, like a bride walking down the aisle of a cathedral on her wedding day. Their boat was out of the slip, and Dorothy and Pastor Cook were standing in the water waiting for me. Wearing my patriotic T-shirt, I stepped down the ladder into the lake and stood between the two of them. Men from the ministry stood on the three-sided dock as ski boats raced by. The warm sun shined on my face as Pastor Cook and Dorothy baptized me. This moment seemed like it was choreographed in heaven. The Lord knew that the Fourth of July was one of my favorite holidays; sunrise and sunset were my favorite times of the day; and the water was my favorite place to be.

♥ *"... For if we died with Him, We shall also live with Him.*
If we endure, we shall also reign with Him,
If we deny Him, He also will deny us"
(2 Timothy 2:11-12).

In the fall of 1993, when new members of Hillcrest Church were being introduced at the Sunday service, I saw one lady standing with the group and felt drawn to her. Regardless of the fact that I was only a visitor at that time, I mustered up the courage and congratulated her for joining the church. She was working at Christ for the Nations Bible School. A few months later, she needed to move closer to North Dallas. I invited her to share my home, and she moved in a week later.

Being an early riser, when I got up I noticed a light under the door of her bedroom and wondered, *What is she doing up so early?*

At breakfast, she told me, "I'm reading my Bible."

My Transformation

I never met anyone who had such dedication to the Lord. She showed me what a real Christian woman was like and became a dear friend and mentor. The aroma from my garden was sweeter because God brought Lauri Schroeder Irion into my life.

In July 1994, she gave me a Bible with my name engraved on it for my birthday. I had a hard time understanding what I was reading. Back then, when people talked about reading the Word, I didn't realize that they were referring to the Bible. Lauri helped me to memorize scripture—the first step for me to truly grow in the Lord. I would write verses on white index cards, such as—"I can do all things through Christ who strengthens me" (Philippians 4:13). I placed them on my bathroom mirror, my refrigerator, and in my car to help me remember the scripture. I continue this practice today.

One gorgeous day, when Lauri came to visit Dallas, we packed a cooler and headed to the Arboretum—beautiful botanical gardens in Dallas displaying an incredible variety of trees, flowers, shrubs, exotic ferns, brooks and waterfalls. With a blanket and Bible in hand, we lined up at the gate and bought our tickets. Something inside me seemed to say, *Turn to the left once you get inside.* We took that path which led us to a bench near a stream in the fern gardens. We sat down and enjoyed the delicate greenery and fragrance of the flowers.

I suggested, "Let's close our eyes, be still, and just listen in silence." For two women who liked to talk, that's quite a chore. We sat for about five minutes, when suddenly, my friend asked me to open my Bible and turn to Deuteronomy 8:7-9. I looked down at my Bible and it was already opened to that exact passage!

♥ *"For the Lord your God is bringing you into a good land, a land of brooks of water, of fountains and springs, that flow out of valleys and hills; a land of wheat and barley, of vines and fig trees and pomegranates, a land of olive oil and honey, a land in which you will eat bread without scarcity, in which you will lack nothing"*
(Deuteronomy 8:7-9).

She Dares to Dream

I felt a new freshness in my spirit. I felt alive and excited but not sure about what. After reading that promise, some wonderful events have taken place in my life. I have had the opportunity to travel to some faraway places—Costa Rica, Scandinavia, Greece, Turkey, Bulgaria, Romania, Alaska, Australia, Israel, Thailand, Brazil, Russia, China and Mexico. God opened doors for me to speak and conduct Bible studies on five-star cruise ships and take mission trips to Third World countries to minister to orphans and people who did not know Jesus. As the scripture told me, *You will lack nothing.*

The splendor of my garden became brighter when Lauri introduced me to another precious woman. She became a prayer partner, a mentor, and a treasured friend. This woman is bold in her prayers, committed to her vision, and tender in her touch. She showed me how to obey God's call when she packed two suitcases, left her entire world, and moved to Kenya, Africa.

Katie Lacadie, Lauri Irion, and Jan Tennyson

She founded the ministry, Rejoice Africa, and served there for fourteen years. Many have come to Christ because of her dedication and commitment to the call on her life. This prayer warrior, Katie Lacadie, gave me a *Women of Destiny Bible* for my birthday in July 2000, with my name and this scripture engraved on the front: *"But you be watchful in all things, endure afflictions, do the work of an evangelist, fulfill your ministry"* (2 Timothy 4:5).

Dan and Sara Lenhart, Jim and Dale Ash, and Hart and Sandra Dinkens became mentors who recognized my potential and tucked me under their wings. They helped me to recognize who I was in Christ. I learned how to move from selfishness

My Transformation

to selflessness, from receiving to giving, and how to rely on the Holy Spirit for direction in my life. I had to reposition my heart, so God could reveal His vision in order to use me for His purposes.

A delicate blossom that I played with as a child was a Forget-me-not. This flower best exemplifies *remembrance* of the person God sent me as a treasured volunteer. For more than twenty years, he served as a member of the Board of Directors of *Dare to Dream* Children's Foundation.

At one event, he said, "I must have had my head stuck in the ground because I had no idea that things were as bad as they are for some children." He often had a twinkle in his eye as he spoke of his *charmed life* growing up with people who loved him. Discovering what the *real* world was like for many youngsters propelled him into speaking on behalf of children when he could, giving finances when he could, and serving however he could. His generosity touched my life and my ministry. He was a refined gentleman who celebrated life and helped many along the way to do the same. My precious Forget-me-not is Jay R. McLure who will long be remembered. He went to heaven in December 2008.

Jan Tennyson and Jay R. McLure

My garden became more complete when another friend gave me a book that I treasure—*God's Generals* by Roberts Lairdon. These fascinating biographies introduced me to some of the most extraordinary heroes of the faith—Aimee Semple McPherson, Smith Wigglesworth, Kathryn Kuhlman, and others. I did not know that God could take ordinary men and women and dramatically empower them through the Holy Spirit to perform the miraculous. God placed this fragrant lily in my life to illustrate firsthand God's incredible healing power in the world today. My friend, healing evangelist, Loretta Blasingame is truly one of God's Generals.

A well-known radio host in Dallas, Tom Dooley, gave me a tape on forgiveness and wrote a note: *To a treasured daughter of a King.* It is the dearest description that I have ever received of how Jesus sees me. He called me *daughter*, which says, *endearing relationship, my offspring.* I no longer felt excluded, but included. Once Jesus met me in my broken and bruised state of mind, he whispered to my spirit—*You belong.*

I am blessed to have pastors, evangelists, Bible scholars, teachers, authors, and many special people who cared enough to share their faith and their friendship. My heavenly father sent visiting angels to care for me when I was sick, friends to encourage me when I was grieving, and laugh with me when I wanted to cry. For each of you, I am eternally grateful.

Lennie Allen was the Hillcrest Church Pastor of World Outreach from 1988-2004. He developed relationships with ministries all over the world. Because of his vision, I was exposed to people at Mission Conferences who were serving God in places I had only dreamed about. When the trip to Israel was announced at my church in 1996, I didn't hesitate to step out of my comfort zone and go.

Jan in Jerusalem on the Mount of Olives

Visiting Israel and walking where Jesus walked changed my life forever. As I was sitting on the shore of the Sea of Galilee reflecting on the scriptures, the Bible came alive. I could now comprehend so much more about what I was reading. I could

My Transformation

hardly contain my tears of joy as a member of our group sang the song, "Jerusalem" during our Sunday service on the Mount of Olives overlooking the city of Jerusalem.

I loosely made a statement to some friends—"If I ever get baptized as an adult, it will take place in the River Jordan where Jesus was baptized." By the grace of God, on June 7, 1996, dressed in a white baptismal robe with the sun shining on my hair, I rededicated my life to Jesus in the River Jordan.

Jan with Rev. Johnny Moffett at the River Jordan, Israel

♥ *"I indeed baptize you with water unto repentance, but He who is coming after me is mightier than I, whose sandals I am not worthy to carry. He will baptize you with the Holy Spirit and fire"* (Matthew 3:11).

The Jesus Video

In 1998, when I was invited on a seventeen-day cruise, I thought, *What an amazing mission field. What a great place to minister to people from all over the world.*

It was an exciting moment as the Crystal Symphony cruise ship pulled out of the port of Los Angeles on the fourteenth of January. I climbed the outside stairs to the top deck and reflected on the faraway places we would be cruising—*Waikiki and Maui in Hawaii, and Samoa and Tonga in the South Pacific, and Auckland, New Zealand.*

The days at sea were my favorite because they allowed me to write parts of this book without distraction in the privacy of my cabin, which had an outdoor balcony. Wearing my white bathrobe each morning, while enjoying breakfast and sipping tea was one of my favorite times of the day. I would read my Bible as the soft wind gently stroked the pages. For me, this was a little piece of heaven on earth.

Each day I met interesting people from faraway places and many times had the opportunity to tell them about Jesus. Admiring the ice carvings displayed at the delicious lunch buffets, attending seminars with famous speakers, and enjoying the fabulous evening entertainment made each day an incredible adventure.

I became friends with a beautiful Christian singer who performed on board. We shared our hopes and dreams as we prayed together on the balcony of my cabin. When I told her about my dream to speak on a cruise ship, she smiled and said she would introduce me to the director who selects the speakers. He just happened to be on board.

We left the room, descended the fabulous winding staircase to the lobby, and walked directly into him. She introduced us, and he was intrigued with my life's work.

After enjoying the first leg of the world cruise, I returned to Dallas to attend an *All About Love* silent auction and dance—a fundraiser for *Dare to Dream* Children's Foundation. I touched base with the volunteers, and had a Valentine's event that was spectacular.

Two weeks later, I received a postcard signed by my new friends who were still cruising around the world.

"We miss you."

"You've been AWOL (absent without leave) for almost two weeks."

"Sydney, Australia, wasn't the same without you."

My Transformation

These people wanted me to return, but I hesitated at first. However, my pastor encouraged me to return to the ship—"Jan, you've dedicated your whole life to serving others, and now you have an opportunity to take advantage of God's abundant blessings. His favor is on you, and it will continue to be on you."

My heart was excited, and I phoned the man who hires the speakers in Los Angeles, California. To my surprise, he answered the phone personally!

"Hello, I'm the *Dare to Dream* lady from Dallas who was introduced to you on the first leg of the Mediterranean Majesty cruise on the Crystal Symphony."

He responded, "Yes, I remember you. I heard a rumor that you'll be returning to the ship."

"I'm not sure about that yet." Instead of asking him about speaking on board, I found myself asking a totally different question.

"Tell me, if I do return to the ship over the Easter holiday, would you be willing to show the *Jesus* film in the Hollywood theatre on Good Friday?"

He immediately said, "Jan, this is the last leg of our journey and everything is already scheduled."

He paused a moment and then said, "Come to think of it, Easter is our cruise director's favorite holiday. Bring the video to the ship and give it to him as soon as you arrive on board."

I knew, then, this trip was to be part of my future.

From April 7 to April 15, 1998, I spent eight glorious days aboard the Crystal Symphony cruise ship from Piraeus, Greece, to Dover, England. Once I arrived on board the ship in Athens, a couple of surprises were waiting for me in my cabin—a gorgeous bouquet of flowers with a note from friends who walked the deck with me at the crack of dawn each morning on the first leg of the trip. And hanging on my closet door was as an "Early Bird Society" sport shirt. As soon as I got settled in, I took the elevator down to the front desk with the *Jesus* video in hand. The receptionist was expecting me and said, "The cruise director has been waiting for this."

When I woke up the next morning, I read the Reflections newsletter that was put under the door of my cabin. What a surprise it was to read, "Good Friday Special—the Life of *Jesus* video repeating every two hours, on the hour—TV channel 35." More than 700 cabins would have an opportunity to see the story of *Jesus*, produced by Campus Crusade for Christ, over the entire Easter weekend! Guests remarked at the dinner table, "Jan, this really made our Easter weekend complete."

After docking in Casablanca, the pianist from the ship invited me to join him for a walk to the Hyatt Regency Hotel to visit the famous café, Joe's Place. He knew I played the piano and was fascinated with the black and white classic movie, *Casablanca*. Hanging from the wall behind the piano was a giant picture of Humphrey Bogart and Ingrid Bergman. We sat together as he played "As Time Goes By" from the celebrated movie. Picturing myself in the film, I closed my eyes and listened to the tune. When he finished the song, I couldn't resist reciting the famous line: "Play it again, Sam."

Jan playing piano in the lobby of the Crystal Symphony cruise ship.

Once we returned to the ship, I was inspired to entertain the guests on the unique glass top piano in the lobby at the bottom of the winding staircase. I felt like a celebrity as guests listened attentively while sipping their cocktails and waiting for the dinner chime to ring. At the magic moment, much like a grand entrance to a dinner party at the palace, people paraded past me to beautifully decorated dinner tables. Guests in their formal attire were eager to enjoy a menu of fine wines, exotic foods, unique desserts, and romantic violin music.

♥ *"Now unto Him that is able to do exceeding abundantly above all that we ask or think, according to the power that worketh in us"*
(Ephesians 3:20 NLT).

A Dream Come True

As we were heading to Bordeaux, France, on the Crystal Symphony, one of my lifelong dreams was about to come true. Walking down the long corridor of the ship to my stateroom, I couldn't help but notice the lovely invitations that were placed on the cabin doors of the world cruisers. They were invited to all kinds of private parties. That gave me an idea—*Why not ask the cruise director if I could have my own private party?* Throughout the journey, whenever a friendship was developed, I asked the passenger for the correct spelling of their name and for their cabin number. This helped build my invitation list just in case an arrangement could be made for me to speak on board. Since stories about sunken treasure were being told on the ship, I selected *"Dare to Dream—Find the Hidden Treasure Within"* as my topic.

The cruise director listened intently as I presented my idea.

"I'd like to have an event on the top deck in the Palm Court." In my opinion this was the most fabulous room on the ship.

"That's fine Jan, but the only slot of time I have open is eight o'clock in the morning."

I said, "Wonderful! I'll take it." Stretching his generosity, I made another request. "It would be terrific if we could have a continental breakfast buffet for the guests before my talk."

He graciously agreed to all my requests! That afternoon, I discovered some cards and envelopes in the ship's library, and a staff person said, "You are welcome to use them for your party." I printed the invitations on the computer and had a butler hand deliver them to each cabin.

The night before I was to speak, dressed in my green sparkling evening gown, I visited the Palm Court. Finding a crewmember, I told him that I would be speaking here early tomorrow morning and asked if it would be possible to place the piano in the middle of the dance floor.

He quickly responded, "We never move the piano."

In spite of his reply, I said, "It would be wonderful if the chairs could be placed in half-moon style surrounding the piano." I smiled and returned to my cabin, praying that it would be set up exactly the way I requested.

Awakening in the wee hours the morning of the event, my throat was terribly sore. Looking at the clock, it was 3:00 a.m. I called the ship's doctor. With chills one minute and a high temperature shortly after, I dragged myself into the elevator and down to the infirmary. The doctor gave me a cortisone shot and I had to lie there for almost an hour. With difficulty, I whispered, "Will I be able to speak at eight o'clock in the morning?"

Reluctantly, he said, "Yes, if you get some rest. But, make sure you come back here immediately after your presentation; you'll need another shot. You have a very bad throat." Feeling totally exhausted, I returned to my cabin at 5:00 a.m.

Determined that this was not going to spoil my dream, with only one hour of sleep I got up and dressed for the big day. Before leaving the cabin, I picked up the Reflections newsletter for Tuesday, April 21, 1998 that was placed under the cabin door. It read: 8:00 a.m. *Dare to Dream*: Fellow guest, Jan Tennyson, gives an informal, inspirational talk in the Palm Court. Wow! I never expected the gathering to be publicized to all the cabins on the ship. I was pleased because it was such an early hour for

My Transformation

passengers to get up, especially since there was a late celebration the night before.

With so little sleep, I slowly managed to get dressed and take the elevator to the Palm Court. I was pleasantly surprised as I walked into the lovely setting. The piano was placed exactly where I wanted it. The chairs were lined up in half-moon rows surrounding the white baby grand, and a scrumptious continental breakfast was available for my guests.

Exhausted, and still having difficulty with my throat, I stood quietly as guests trickled in about ten minutes before my talk. A nurse who was helping greet the guests asked, "Jan, you still can't talk. How do you expect to pull this off?"

Jan in the Palm Court on a Crystal Symphony cruise.

I said, "Please, let's step aside and pray." When we finished, a fellow passenger, a golf professional, introduced me. Smiling as I walked towards the piano, I played and spoke for forty-five minutes as clear as if nothing was wrong. The presentation was well received and God was honored. As soon as the thirty guests left the Palm Court, my throat closed again. I returned to the infirmary for another shot.

"What did you speak about?" the doctor asked.

I told the doctor that I challenge audiences to *Dare to Dream* and find the hidden treasure within. By the look on his face, it was evident that he was interested in knowing more. Since we were traveling during the Easter season, I said that I had been passing out the *Jesus* video to people in each port.

"If you promise to watch this great story, I'll give you a copy to take home to your country." He thanked me and promised to take it to his homeland in Norway.

Crossing the English Channel on April 24, 1998 enroute to Dover, England, where we would disembark, saddened my heart. This wonderful mission/cruise trip was coming to an end. The "Early Bird" world cruisers honored me with a going-away party including cards, gifts, and many good wishes.

It was a privilege for me to put the story of the greatest Man who ever lived into the hands of so many people from around the world. The ship departed on its Routes of Royalty itinerary—Piraeus, Greece; Kusadasi, Turkey; Valletta, Malta; Naples, Italy; Palma de Mallorca; Barcelona and Cadiz, Spain; Casablanca, Morocco; Lisbon, Portugal; Bordeaux, France, and Dover, England. I disembarked the ship feeling like a princess who just had a dream come true. My heart said, *Mission Accomplished.*

♥ *"Keep me as the apple of Your eye;*
Hide me under the shadow of Your wings..."
(Psalm 16:8).

The Great Commission

One morning, while viewing some beautifully framed scriptures in the Gallery at Hillcrest Church, I stood frozen in my tracks as I read—"Go into all the world and preach the Gospel to every creature" (Mark 16:15). Tears that I could not explain began running down my face. I felt that as sure as the seasons on the earth were changing, the direction in which God was calling me was changing. That day, the Lord put a hunger in my heart to go to the nations, and He orchestrated every step of the way.

♥ *"May I never be ashamed of the gospel, O Lord, for it is the power of God to salvation for everyone who believes..."* (From Romans 1:16).

A Miracle in Turkey

Hearing a report on television about a devastating earthquake in Turkey, I telephoned my foster sister Cookie to find out if she and her family were safe. By the grace of God, it didn't destroy anything in Balikesir, where she lived. On the Internet, I found the following report in a Turkish newspaper:

"A major earthquake took place in Turkey August 17, 1999, at 3:02 a.m. local time, waking the majority of people from their sleep. It was accompanied by significant aftershocks and many apartment buildings, in the poorest section of Izmet collapsed burying thousands. In Gulcuk, sixty miles from Istanbul, about 500 buildings collapsed burying many people alive. Approximately 248 sailors died on a Turkish naval base. Survivors felt intense helplessness because they could hear people who were trapped calling for help, but they were unable to rescue them from the rubble. Turkish soldiers were given 45 days leave to help rescue their relatives. Bodies were buried quickly in mass graves to stop any spread of disease."

CNN reported more than 14,000 dead and 200,000 homeless. In an instant, lives were changed forever.

I told Cookie, "I'll be traveling with my friend, Loretta, and our cruise ship will dock overnight in Istanbul. We would like you to make arrangements for us to go to the earthquake zones and visit the survivors."

She told me that it would never happen and that the camps were off limits especially to an American Christian woman. I was aware of the persecution of Christians in that part of the world, but I put my fears behind and prayed that the Lord would prepare the way. The Bible tells us—

> ♥ *"Have I not commanded you? Be strong and of a good courage; do not be afraid, nor be dismayed, for the Lord your God is with you wherever you go"*
> (Joshua 1:9).

Once the cruise ship arrived in Istanbul, Cookie met us in a taxi. She was bursting with excitement. "Janice, you won't believe what I'm about to tell you. A friend's son, who lived through the earthquake, is a dentist in the military and is assigned to a survivors tent camp in Gulcuk. He has made arrangements for us to visit the camp!"

Thankful for the news, I knew that the Lord had paved the way for the miraculous to happen that day. After breakfast with Cookie on the ship, we began our adventure to one of the largest survivor camps in Turkey. I wondered nervously, *What would we find there? How could we help?*

What we did not know was that this would be a four-legged journey that would take enormous coordination. The wild taxi ride to the ferry with our Turkish driver was an amazing experience all on its own. How our cab fit through the narrow streets at such high speeds without hitting any pedestrians along the way, was a mystery. Arriving safely at the waterfront, Loretta, Cookie, and I boarded a crowded ferry to cross the Bosphorus—also known as the Golden Horn—a body of water leading to the Black Sea. Smelling the scents of the sea, with the sound of Turkish music coming from the shore, and watching the anxious expressions on the faces of mothers, children, workers, and students was like we were in the middle of a movie, with important roles to play. My heart went out to the families; some of them searching for loved ones wondering, *Where is my husband? Is my little girl safe?*

My Transformation

Not knowing what the future would hold that day, with a dream in our hearts and a prayer on our lips, we were determined to keep going.

Arriving on the opposite side of the waterway, we exited the ferry and walked a short distance on a dusty street to a local bus that took us to our next stop. With a heavy heart, I peered out of the windows, passing survivors living in tents along the roadway. After the one-hour bus ride, Cookie guided us to an old white van waiting for us down the street. It definitely had seen better days, but we were thankful to have transportation. Without windows to look out, or seats to sit on, it was an uncomfortable bumpy ride on the hard metal floor all the way to the camp. We were relieved when we heard the driver say, "This is the last leg of your trip. You'll soon be at the camp." Having Cookie interpret the language was a tremendous blessing!

After the forty-five-minute ride, we came to an abrupt halt. The side of the van slid open and right before our eyes were uniformed Turkish soldiers holding rifles guarding the area. The soldier, who had made it possible for our visit, was waiting and warmly guided us though the camp. He gave us every courtesy that one would bestow to dignitaries arriving on foreign soil, and our fears were relieved. Walking past rows and rows of blue tents, we saw mostly women and children. Stopping along the way listening to their heartbreaking stories, I had to hold my emotions in check. I was here to comfort, not to cry.

Each day, people were clinging to the hope that a relative or friend would be discovered alive in the rubble of what were once five-and-six-story buildings. Some were reunited with loved ones, but many would never see their families again. As we walked through the camp, little children were drawn to the American flag T-shirt I was wearing and timidly reached for my outstretched hand. Our presence provided a brief, but hopeful break to their days of sadness. As children gathered around, listening and watching every move we made, one sweet woman, Ayse, invited us into her tent for hot tea and cookies. Cookie ventured off to buy candy for some children, leaving Loretta and me without a translator.

In spite of our inability to speak the language, music bridged the gap between our cultures. We began singing "Deep in the Heart of Texas." When I began singing "My Bonnie Lies Over the Ocean," it was amazing to me that they knew the song! Gesturing to the young woman sitting across from me to sing for us, she shyly smiled and lowered her head. Eventually, she began singing Turkish songs, and everyone joined in.

We reunited with Cookie. As she passed out candy to the children, I asked her, "Who do these people think we are?"

"I told them you are praying women."

A few moments later, a lady boldly walked up to us and told Cookie her baby was having trouble breathing. The baby was wheezing badly and the mother wanted us to pray. I looked at Loretta and said, "Do we dare? Do we dare lay hands on this baby and pray regardless of the warnings that Christians were being killed for expressing their faith?" Without hesitation, I answered my own question. "What a way to go!" The mother handed the baby to me and we prayed, claiming healing in the name of Jesus. We placed the child back in his mother's arms. About an hour later, she came running up to us smiling from ear to ear, and again handed me her son. His breathing was perfectly clear.

Jan and Loretta Blasingame 1999.

A miracle took place that day in a Turkish survivors camp because we were willing to *go into all the world*, and believe that God's Word is true.

We began our long journey back to the ship, where Cookie stayed overnight in our cabin. Before she returned to her home in Balikesir the next day, she asked for prayer to receive the baptism of the Holy Spirit. Our prayers were answered, and my sweet foster sister who shared a bedroom with me when we were little girls, received the fullness of God and now knew and experienced the power of the Holy Spirit.

Cookie was orphaned as an infant and grew up in the Brennan's home. She has become an educated woman in a faraway place teaching English to Turkish students and translating in an earthquake zone. I am so proud of her.

Our roles were fulfilled that day as heaven orchestrated a miraculous event in a place where we were willing to go in the name of the Lord. Three American women came together to bring smiles to sad faces and joy to the children by speaking the language of love.

> ♥ *"Most assuredly, I say to you, he who believes in me, the works that I do, he will do also; and greater works than these he will do, because I go to the Father"*
> (John 14:12).

The Army of God in Romania

Jan visiting a hospital in Romania

My first trip to Romania was with an organization called Humanity United in Giving (HUG), founded by Judy Broom. Her incredible work, improving the lives of innocent babies, gave me the opportunity to visit orphanages and hospitals housing hundreds of children.

On my second trip to Romania in May 2002, I was invited by Christ Commission for Romania, and led a team from Dallas, Texas, to the orphanages, nursing homes, and churches in Timisoara, Romania. We visited a Life Center that housed young men who had lived in orphanages since infancy. The first night, our team sang with the orphans "Spirit of the living God," and "I Surrender All." By showing them the love of Christ in our words and our actions, all the orphan boys at the center invited Christ to live in their hearts that evening.

The following week, I invited them to sing praise music before I spoke in the auditorium at the mid-week service at the Christ for the Nations Bible School.

"Do you really mean it? We never have been asked to sing in front of an audience before," one boy remarked. They got haircuts, put on their best clothing, and sang their hearts out. Perhaps for the first time in their lives, they felt really important. The audience loved them. Their faith and belief in a living God was strengthened that evening, and they now had a new melody of hope in their hearts.

On another occasion, the Christ for the Nations' students, who lived a short distance from The Life Center where the orphans lived, asked our mission group from Dallas to join them to minister in a resort park. People from all over the world come to visit this beautiful place. I agreed, but was a little uneasy since I had never done street ministry before. Walking through the lovely park to the gazebo, while students strummed their guitars, made one think that something important was about to take place.

One of the Romanian pastors introduced himself to the crowd and said a few words. Then he surprised me and asked, "Miss Jan, would you please say something to the visitors?" With my heart pounding as the music stopped, I slowly walked and stood next to the pastor silently praying, *Holy Spirit, please help me and put words into my mouth just like you did for Moses.*

My Transformation

I stepped out towards the crowd standing on the other side of the path and said, "I believe God sent me all the way from Dallas, Texas, for this special moment in time. I'm not a Dallas Cowboy cheerleader, but I am a cheerleader for Jesus, and it is an honor to have the opportunity to speak with you today." The crowd smiled as the translator spoke my words. "What you are looking at across this path are students who are spending the most precious years of their lives studying what this book has to say."

I held up my Bible and walked over to the visitors and said, "For most of my life I was on this side of the street, not knowing much about this book. But I could see joy in the eyes of people who knew God, and I wanted that. I began studying and, although it has taken a long time, I have learned how to enter the peace of His presence. What you are looking at across this path is the Army of God."

I walked back across the path and said to our group, "I'd like you to stand in one long line, shoulder-to-shoulder, like you are on the front lines of a battlefield." Students, pastors, orphans from the Life Center, and my Dallas team, stood as straight as an arrow like soldiers ready for war. I then walked into the crowd of visitors and encouraged them.

"If you would like to become a member of God's army and learn about the peace, love, and joy that only Jesus can bring, line up on this side of the path shoulder-to-shoulder and face God's army." By the power of the Holy Spirit, they followed my orders as though they were listening to a four-star General.

I asked the students to extend their right hand across the path to the people standing opposite them. Visitors were asked to do the same. "Now take one step forward and touch the hand of the person opposite you. And when you touch the person's hand, it will be like touching the hand of God. Now pray together, release your burdens, love one another and change your life forever."

The power of God was present. People were getting saved, marriages were being restored, people were getting healed, children were praying, orphans were speaking scriptures they had never spoken before, and God was glorified.

I walked a short distance away, leaned against a tree and wept...

A Candle in Thailand

Jan ministering to Burmese children in a refugee camp in Thailand

In 2001, my friend, Mary Dunham Faulkner, founder of Leah's Sisters, invited me to join her team to speak to Burmese students in a refugee camp in Thailand. Holding an unlit candle and speaking the words of an old hymn, I said, "It only takes a spark to get a fire going; and soon all those around will warm up to its glowing. That's how it is with God's love once you experience it. It's fresh like spring, you want to sing, and you want to pass it on."

I passed the unlit candle on to their teacher and told her that I would remember our time together always. The joyful look in the eyes of the children as I encouraged them made me feel that I had given them hope. The candle represented the light that you and I bring into a dark world when we tell wounded people about the love of God.

♥ *"Your Word is a lamp to my feet and a light to my path"* (Psalm119:105).

A Banquet Table in Russia —

As a six-year-old child in Sacred Heart Grammar School in Bayside, each day my class prayed with the nuns for the salvation of Russia.

Over fifty years later, in 2003, I prayed again at a Sunday service while sitting on a cruise ship in Russian waters. I thanked God that my prayers had been answered.

Three years later, on a mission trip in March 2006, more prayers were prayed in the home of a Russian foster mother who had invited some of our team members for a delicious dinner. Some wonderful student translators helped us get acquainted. While eating dessert, I ministered to the foster mother, and that evening she invited Christ into her life. Again, our prayers from so long ago were answered.

During the week, some of our team from Dallas ministered to forty-five Russian orphans who were exiting the system. Before going to Russia, a manual was developed to help orphans identify a purpose and vision for their lives. Once we got acquainted, it was an honor to present each student with a copy of our *Dare to Dream* booklet translated for them into the Russian language. When I asked them to put their name on the book, one boy said, "You mean this is mine for keeps?"

The students learned a prayer for a vision and a prayer that would help them learn to forgive those who hurt them. Topics dealing with money management, communication skills, and manners were also included.

Having grown up in the foster care system, I had a platform in which the young people could identify. Discussing the disadvantages of holding on to a victim mentality hopefully helped them to work on the fear factor of their lives. I encouraged them to learn about the power of the Holy Spirit, which was new to them. I told them that the *Bible* is the doorway to a new way of thinking, and that they could do all things through Christ who would give them strength. I encouraged them to memorize scripture. Helping them prepare for the world outside of an orphanage was a role that I welcomed, but never dreamed I would have.

Before leaving Dallas to come on this trip, I wanted to have a banquet for the orphans who were exiting the system. Because there would be no families to greet them or tell them how much they were loved, creating an experience they would never forget was my dream. Having a banquet table with the finest food, china, and silverware in a beautiful setting was the desire of my heart. Jesus broke bread with his disciples at the Last Supper, and I wanted our team to break bread with the orphans before they exited the orphanage for the outside world.

The night before we left for America, and with the help of many caring volunteers, our special evening took place. It was at the hotel where we were staying in Vladimir, located on the Klyzama River, 200 kilometers (124 miles) east of Moscow.

Smiling orphans, looking tall and proud, dressed in their finest outfits, marched into the room and found their seats at the U shaped banquet table. The Russian Flag and the American Flag were crossed as the centerpiece and strategically placed. The formal meal was served on white china dinner plates, with shiny silverware meticulously placed on the bright red table napkins. Watching the teenagers and our team sitting together, bowing their heads and saying grace before the meal was emotional for me. I remembered how long ago I had prayed for a day that God would be honored in Russia.

During the meal several orphans stood up and expressed gratitude for our time together, and when we finished eating I presented each person with a small card showing Jesus standing at a door inviting a lonely man to His banquet table. A prayer, printed on the back of the card, in the Russian language read:

There is a door to your heart, and Jesus is knocking on it. He won't open it against your will. He wants to lead you through the door to the Father's house in Heaven. Will you open your heart to Him and receive His invitation?

I asked them to put the card in a book that would help them remember our evening together at our banquet table with the King.

> "I am the door. If anyone enters by Me, he will be saved, and will go in and out and find pasture. The thief does not come except to steal, and to kill, and to destroy. I have come that they may have life, and that they may have it more abundantly" (John 10:9,10).

In missionary Colton Wickramaratne's book, *My Adventure in Faith*, he states, "Never give up. If you are moving in God's plan, there is no man on earth, no force in the universe, no demon in hell that can frustrate or destroy the plan of God concerning you."

It seems like yesterday that I traveled to Costa Rica on a mission trip, when I didn't even know what that was. At the time, I was just beginning to learn about reading the Bible and practicing my faith. On that trip I shared my dream to help unfortunate children have a better life. Little did I know then, that God was giving me just a snapshot of a journey that had only just begun.

In the chapters to follow, you will read faith-filled adventure stories that I hope will leave you wanting to pick up a pen and paper and write your own life story.

> ♥ *"Those who are wise will shine like the brightness of the heavens, and those who lead many to righteousness, like the stars forever and ever"*
> (Daniel 12:3 NIV).

Chapter Twelve

Wow Stories

Here is a snapshot of some amazing experiences that impacted my life and warmed my heart once I decided to live a life of service to the Lord.

The Sound of Music

In the mid-eighties, a prayer group from Hillcrest church met in my home twice a month. One evening we were standing in a circle in my living room speaking our prayer requests one by one. When it was my turn, I began praying for my two children. Suddenly, I heard music coming from the kitchen area. The music box on the top of my refrigerator, which I hadn't wound up in years, started playing the song, "Do-Re-Mi" from the musical "The Sound of Music." The group was flabbergasted!

When my children were very young, their dad bought the music box for them to give to me for Mother's Day. It was a statue of a mom, wearing a long dress with an apron, holding an iron in her hand. I believe the music was a sign to me that Jesus hears my every prayer, and is holding my children in the palm of His hand.

A Rocket Ship to Heaven

One day in my office, I was telling a friend about an incident concerning my spiritual journey.

"Most of my life I attended church; but in 1993 when I had an amazing encounter with the Holy Spirit, it was like taking a *rocket ship to heaven*. My face got warm and it seemed like a light bulb had been turned on inside of me. I looked at the world with different eyes. My desires changed, my speech changed, and my heart was more compassionate."

Remarkably, a few days later, a *Dare to Dream* volunteer walked into my office and said, "Something in my spirit told me to give you this picture."

This gift was a picture of a rocket ship taking off, and under the flames from the exhaust were the words *Dare to Dream*. The volunteer never heard me say the words—*rocket ship to heaven*. That extraordinary picture hangs in the *Dare to Dream* Children's Foundation office and reminds me that God is faithful and confirms what he has called me to do.

A Final Home Run

As a teenager growing up in New York, Mickey Mantle was the greatest! The fans loved this slugging center fielder of the New York Yankees during the 1950s and 1960s. His baseball feats and golden good looks made him an American legend.

I wasn't much of a sports fan, but when he moved to Dallas, I became interested in his accomplishments. In early 1995, while watching the news on TV, it was reported that Mickey had liver cancer. I was concerned about his illness, but I was more concerned about his spiritual well being. Because he was known as quite a party guy in his day, I began praying for his salvation.

Several years later, at the Infomart in Dallas, I had a trade show booth and was distributing materials to the public about *Dare to Dream*. After the event, a woman in the next booth asked, "Would you like to have this balloon bouquet for some children?"

I thanked her and said, "The Casa kids will love them." After dropping it off, I passed Lovers Lane United Methodist Church on Northwest Highway on the way back to my office. Cars were parked everywhere. Suddenly I remembered hearing the radio report that Mickey Mantle had died, and his funeral service was being held at that church.

A few weeks earlier at a news conference, Mickey gave a surprising message to his fans: "I'm no role model for America's youth. Don't be like me. God gave me a great body to play with, and I didn't take care of it. I blame a lot of it on alcohol."

It isn't often that a person has a chance to deliver a message like that, but I'm glad he did. I decided to attend his funeral and drove around a five-block area, but couldn't find a parking spot anywhere. Discouraged, I started to go back to my office. But, after driving four blocks past the church, a voice inside me said, *Turn this car around!* Without hesitation, I made a U-turn and drove directly into the church parking lot.

Noticing an orange cone that marked an empty spot right next to a large black limousine parked in front of the church, I asked the driver, "Is that spot reserved for someone?" Smiling, he replied, "I believe it's reserved just for you ma'am." He removed the cone and motioned for me to take the best place in the lot.

After I pushed open the door to the lobby, an usher greeted me and said, "The main sanctuary is overflowing, but the Fellowship Hall still has some room."

As soon as I walked through the door, the pastor announced on the wide-screen: "I'm honored to tell you that Mickey accepted Jesus as his Lord and Savior when I was with him in the hospital. He is in heaven now." I cried when I heard the news. That's all I wanted to know! My prayers had been answered.

SHE DARES TO *Dream*

The service was over, and I got up and slowly walked towards the guest book. Picking up the pen, I wrote, Jan Tennyson—*Dare to Dream*. I was the last person to sign Mickey Mantle's guest book.

In 1974 he was elected to the Baseball Hall of Fame, and on August 13, 1995, Mickey made his final home run right into the arms of Jesus.

ONE IN A MILLION

On my birthday in July 2004, my brother Gene and I ventured into New York City to visit Ground Zero, the memorial site where the Twin Towers of the World Trade Center were blown apart by terrorists on September 11, 2001. With heavy hearts, we approached the hole in the ground having difficulty imagining that this was the spot where two buildings once stood majestically towering over the New York City skyline.

Years before, I had met with the manager of the fabulous restaurant, "Windows of the World." The view from the top of the towers was spectacular and perfect for a *Dare to Dream* affair. I wanted to invite youngsters from the New York Foundling Home to enjoy lunch with me in a private room. The manager was interested, but now it will never happen.

Gene and I strolled a few blocks to the Bank of America International building across from the Stock Exchange on Broad Street reminiscing. We both worked there when we were in our twenties. To our disappointment, we discovered that the strategic building with its high columns, shiny elevators, and international atmosphere, was now a simple clothing store.

Roaming past the Stock Exchange, Wall Street, and the famous old Trinity Church, which held its first service in 1698, I recalled the days when I would meet my foster dad for lunch in the area. We would stroll through the church graveyard, surrounded by a black wrought-iron fence, glancing at the names on the gravestones.

Gene and I walked downtown to Battery Park and enjoyed refreshments in a large café overlooking the fabulous harbor. The temperature was cool and the sunlight warmed my face. The majestic Statue of Liberty, Governor's Island, and Ellis Island could be seen in the distance.

Jan with brother Gene - July 8, 2004

The park's web site states: "The Battery is one of New York City's oldest public open spaces. Located at the tip of Manhattan overlooking New York Harbor, the Battery hosted Dutch settlers when they came to Manhattan Island and established New Amsterdam. Now it is truly the cradle of New York history, the front lawn of the Downtown district, and a hub of harbor access and cultural tourism. Over four million people, including residents, office workers, school groups, and tourists from around the world annually visit the park and its major landmark, Castle Clinton National Monument."

We purchased our tickets and scurried on to the Staten Island ferry to tour these wonderful sites. Cruising close to the tall lady with the cool sea air blowing, I thought of the thousands of people who came from so far just to get a glimpse of her.

Walking through the doors of the Ellis Island Museum, I wondered if any of my ancestors came to this very place to find a new life in America. Putting on earphones and listening to the voices of people telling their stories about leaving their homeland was touching. Tears spilled from my eyes as I imagined the courage it must have taken to travel across the ocean with their little ones to fulfill a dream for a better life in America. We walked from room to room, looking at photographs of the doctors examining families to make sure they were not bringing disease into our country. It was sad that some families had to be separated because of illness. They were put on a boat and sent back to their homeland.

Returning to Manhattan, we stepped off the ferry and strolled through Battery Park with its variety of artists and photographers from all over the world. After purchasing some treasures, we hailed a taxi to Greenwich Village in lower Manhattan for dinner.

It was a historic moment as we ate in a small Italian sidewalk café on the corner of Perry Street—the block where our father and his brother lived after they were released from the Mount Loretto orphanage. After enjoying a delicious Italian feast, we leisurely walked along that picturesque street with its brownstone houses and tall trees with colorful flowers planted at their bases. How I wished I could turn back the hands of time to see my father running down that street or playing ball with his brother Eddie.

After walking around Greenwich Village, we caught a cab to Pennsylvania Station, commonly called Penn Station. I got out of the car and quickly discovered that I had left my purse with my money, credit cards, and cell phone on the seat! Immediately, I turned and ran towards the cab, but it was too late. He had already pulled away from the curb and was driving up Sixth Avenue. With a feeling of panic, I viewed a sea of yellow cabs, but it was impossible to know which one was ours.

Recalling only the last three numbers on top of the cab, I asked several people, "May I borrow your phone to call my cell phone? I just lost my purse."

"Dream on lady!" one person scoffed. "This is New York City and chances of getting your purse back are one in a million." Discouraged but not defeated, I ran to another driver and asked to borrow his phone to make a report to the taxi company. He graciously gave me some telephone numbers, but none of them could accept my call because the lines were overloaded.

"What are ya gonna do now?" Gene yelled.

"The only thing I know to do is to pray."

He shook his head as I took his hands, and right in front of Penn Station, across the street from Madison Square Garden, we bowed our heads and I prayed: *"Dear Lord, you know exactly where my purse is. Please lead me by your Spirit to find it within this hour, and you will receive the honor and glory in Jesus name. Amen."*

I asked another young man in the station if I could use his phone to make one last call to my cell phone.

He asked, "What's the number?" He made the call and we were both astonished when someone answered!

A man named Mark said, "I picked up the purse from the back seat of the cab and have it with me at the restaurant where I'm eating dinner."

He got the address of the restaurant and I told him that our outfits were red, white, and blue. We quickly hopped in a cab and headed that way. As we got closer to the restaurant on Seventh Avenue, Gene shouted with amazement, "I don't believe it! Look at the name of the restaurant—*The Miracle Grill!*"

Walking inside, the bartender recognized us by our patriotic colors and handed me my purse. I was ecstatic—nothing was missing, but Mark had already left. And just as I prayed, it was found within one hour.

I never got to meet the kind, honest man who found my purse—perhaps he was an angel. I believe this all happened because the Lord wanted Gene to witness the power of prayer and the incredible power of the Holy Spirit.

When we arrived home, he remarked, "I can't wait to tell this *one-in-a-million* story to my airline buddies."

♥ *"...With men this is impossible, but with God all things are possible"* (Matthew 19:26).

She Dares to Dream

A Vision in the Clouds

In March 2005, my sister, Peggy, was suddenly diagnosed with fourth stage of a very aggressive pancreatic cancer—the worst you can have. As soon as I heard the news, I flew to Boca Raton, Florida, to spend some quality time with her.

Early each morning, I drove to the ocean with my Bible on the seat and Peggy's beach chair and umbrella in the trunk. One particular morning, the ocean was calmer and more beautiful than I had seen it in a long time. While reading some scriptures, my cell phone rang and it was my daughter, Lisa, in Atlanta. We chatted as I walked waste deep into the ocean, and then she announced,

"Mom, I have some news for you. David has an offer to take a two-year assignment in Beijing, China."

I was silent for a moment and asked, "Do you think he'll accept the position?"

"It's a once-in-a-lifetime opportunity, and I think we are going to take it. Madeline will get to learn Chinese and attend a school with youngsters from all over the world."

After a short pause, I said, "Sweetheart, if you believe this is what you are supposed to do, you have my blessing."

"I'll let you know what we decide, but it will have to be quickly; they want us there in a month or so."

After the unexpected call, I walked slowly out of the ocean to the beach chair, put my phone down, and then went back into the clear, calm water thinking, *Atlanta is only a two-hour plane trip away, but... across the ocean to China?* I floated on my back, closed my eyes and prayed: *Lord, if this is Your will for my family to live in China, give me a sign so that I'll know this is Your plan for them.*

After reclining on the water a few minutes, I opened my eyes. The white clouds had made a formation looking just like the face of Jesus! Blinking back the tears, I felt the love of God holding me. Normally, a cloud does not stay in the exact same spot for very long. So I closed my eyes thinking, *Perhaps I just imagined the vision.* After a few minutes went by, I opened my eyes and saw the same image in the clouds—the face of Jesus looking back at me.

Driving away from the beach that day, I had perfect peace and assurance that moving to China *was* God's plan for my daughter and her family.

♥ *"And they went out and preached everywhere, the Lord working with them and confirming the word through the accompanying signs"*
(Mark 16:20).

Think of a Rainbow

Each morning, my sister Peggy watched me step out onto the patio at my niece Jeanie's home in Florida. I sat in a quiet place next to the swimming pool and read my Bible. At breakfast one day, I acknowledged her brave fight against pancreatic cancer and said, "If things don't go the way we would like, I don't want you to be afraid. I want you to think of a rainbow."

With a puzzled look on her face, she asked, "A rainbow? Why should I think of a rainbow?"

I smiled and told her, "It's a promise of God's covenant between heaven and earth. We can read about it in the book of Genesis."

"Show me," she said. This was the first time she wanted me to read something out of the Bible to her.

♥ *"This is the sign of the covenant which I make between me and you, and every living creature that is with you, for perpetual generations: I set My rainbow in the cloud, and it shall be for the sign of the covenant between Me and the earth"*
(Genesis 9:12-13).

Another morning, I asked her if she wanted to ask Jesus to come into her heart, and she did.

In spite of her illness, she could still get around pretty well. So I suggested we invite a few of her friends to our favorite spot on the ocean—The Holiday Inn in Highland Beach. Peg loved music and mustered up the strength to join her friends. I walked into the room with Peggy on my arm, and our brother Gene, who was in town, also joined us.

We listened to a few tunes when suddenly, a vicious storm raged over the ocean. The palm trees swayed nearly touching the ground, and we wondered if we were going to have to evacuate the hotel. Remarkably, after about fifteen minutes, the storm calmed and the largest rainbow I'd ever seen spread its colors across the ocean. Peggy jumped up from her chair, grabbed her camera, and said, "Jan, look at that rainbow!" She ran to the outside patio and snapped pictures of the amazing sight.

In my heart, I knew that the Lord was going to take her soon. Within a week and a half on July 13, 2005, Peggy died. She was sixty-seven.

My Gift from the Sea

November 2007 marked the twenty-year anniversary of *Dare to Dream* Children's Foundation. My plans were to put on a celebration to thank everyone who partnered with me through the years. But, one of life's interruptions prevented that from happening. A phone call from my niece, Debbie, in New York changed everything.

"Aunt Jan, my Dad is in the hospital and has cancer." With a broken heart, I quickly packed to leave to be at the bedside of my younger brother, Gene. My flight schedule was from Dallas to Islip, Long Island, with a two-hour layover in Chicago. The weather reports were awful, and the New York airports were covered with ice.

During my layover in Chicago, a lady waiting for the same plane asked me, "Why are you traveling to Long Island?" When I told her, she asked, "Would you mind if I got a few of our church people together to pray with you here at the airport?" I was comforted and knew that the arms of Jesus were surrounding me. Standing in a circle, we bowed our heads and prayed.

One morning I drove Gene's car to Robert Moses State Park. When I walk the beach with the ocean waves crashing in the distance, I find comfort and peace. This particular day was Peggy's birthday, April 11.

My heart was breaking because I had lost my sister not long ago, and now my brother was in the hospital with the same disease. That day, the beach was awesome—no seaweed, no seashells, no footprints, and then, something incredible happened! About ten feet in front of me, I saw an object wash up from the ocean onto the beach. Bending down and picking it up, to my amazement, it was a white porcelain rock in the exact formation of a heart! It was one of those rare and precious moments that almost took my breath away. A tear dropped on my cheek, and I realized that Jesus saw my heart that morning and was letting me know that He was holding me in the palm of His hand. One of my most treasured possessions is that precious gift from the sea.

> ♥ *"Lift up your eyes all around and see: They all gather together, they come to you. Your sons shall come from afar, and your daughters shall be nursed by your side. Then you shall see and become radiant, and your heart will swell with joy; Because the abundance of the sea shall be turned to you..."*
> (Isaiah 60:4, 5).

During an early morning visit to Gene in the hospital, he said, "Isn't it a shame that I had to get cancer to stop drinking?" He was an alcoholic and had been in and out of substance abuse programs for years. He rededicated his life to Christ that day.

A few weeks after I returned to Dallas, Debbie, his daughter, had prepared her home to take care of my brother while he was on hospice. She told him, "Dad, you can smoke cigarettes again, and you can drink whenever you want to."

He shook his head, "Debbie, I don't want to do that anymore."

I've waited a lifetime to hear him say those words.

Once I arrived at MacArthur airport in Long Island, New York, I received a phone call telling me that Gene had just passed away. I got to his home ten minutes after he died—June 27, 2007.

Gene was a Marine and was buried with military honors at Calverton Cemetery, Long Island, New York. He was 63.

A Graveside Savior

All my life, I've been drawn to the tender picture of Jesus sitting with little children on His lap or at His feet. I have often thought, *When I go to heaven, I'd like a statue of that scene placed on my gravesite or memorial garden.* For years, I've searched through catalogues, cemeteries, and art galleries to find one, but to no avail.

However, one day after visiting a friend in Long Island, I passed an exit on the expressway that read "Pinelawn Cemetery." I remembered that was the place where my foster parents are buried. I turned off the road and entered the grounds, but it was a holiday weekend and the information office was closed. In spite of the fact that it was more than twenty years since I had been there, I decided to search for their gravesite. I didn't find it. Reluctantly, I drove back to the main road and headed back to the expressway.

I drove just a few blocks from the grounds and something told me to turn my car around. Across the street from Pinelawn Cemetery, there was a sign that read, St. Charles Cemetery. I realized, *That's it! That's where they're buried.* I entered the park and tried to find the gravesite. As I was driving through the grounds, I found something I didn't expect. In the distance was a large statue of Jesus with little children in His arms and at His feet! I parked my car and slowly walked toward it.

There was a young mother putting flowers on a grave. I asked her about the stuffed toys that were placed at the feet of Jesus. She told me, "This area is sectioned off for babies that have died at birth."

"Do you have a child buried here?"

She responded sadly, "Yes, it was twenty years ago and it seems like it was yesterday."

I held her tenderly in my arms and whispered in her ear, "If you have accepted Jesus in your heart, you'll see your little one again when you get to heaven." I paused a moment and asked, "Is He in your heart?" She looked up at me and whispered, "I hope so."

I then realized that she wasn't sure that she'd go to heaven when she died. Taking a bold step, I said, "If you'd like, I'll lead you in a prayer that will give you the assurance of eternal life. Would you like to pray a prayer to invite Jesus into your heart?"

"Oh yes, I would!" At the gravesite of her little baby, she bowed her head and asked Jesus to forgive her sins and live in her heart. She said she would follow Him all the days of her life. The woman wept with joy and said, "Thank you so much for speaking to me today." We embraced and went our separate ways.

I almost didn't drive into the cemetery that day, but the Holy Spirit guided me, and I obeyed.

♥ *"Love one another, as I have loved you"*
(John 15:12).

The Great Wall of China

Daughter, Lisa and Jan at the Great Wall of China – 2008

In all my travels, China was not on my list of places to visit, but I'm glad I did. Since my son-in-law had an assignment there that lasted nearly four years, I thought that I might miss something if I didn't go. Before the 2008 Olympics, I visited my family in Beijing and learned a little history at the same time. When I found out that my granddaughter, Madeline, camped out with her girl scouts at the Great Wall, I thought, *What a unique experience for a ten year old.*

After Shanghai, Beijing is China's second largest city in terms of population. The China National Radio reported in February 2010 that Beijing's total population has exceeded 22 million.

The Great Wall was built, rebuilt and maintained by various dynasties—the current and the most famous one being built by the Ming dynasty. It was constructed in phases, from fifth century BC to 16th century AD, to protect against attacks from the Mongols. They were an obscure people who lived in the outer reaches of the Gobi Desert in what is now Outer Mongolia. This 6500 kms wonder, also nicknamed the longest tomb, has buried thousands of men while building the wall. One article I read indicated 700,000 workers died.

During my visit, it was a pleasure to meet my daughter's Chinese language instructor. My granddaughter, Madeline, attended the Western Academy of Beijing and was also learning Chinese. As we toured the school, the variety of nations represented and the quality of curriculum being taught was remarkable. I walked into the gym with my daughter and granddaughter as the American flag was being hoisted to the ceiling and our National Anthem was being played—quite a sight for this visitor to Beijing. A badminton tournament had just ended, and the winner was a Chinese-American student.

I loved the people, the food, and watching my family communicate in Chinese. The highlight of my trip was walking the Great Wall of China with Lisa, David, and Madeline—three generations! When visiting the Great Wall, in the interest of preservation, we are asked not to leave behind anything besides our footsteps and take away nothing more than our memories.

I am grateful that my family had the courage to go to a faraway place without knowing the people, the language, or where they were going to live. That day at the ocean when Lisa called and told me about the possibility of moving to China, my heart sank. However, I know it was God's plan, and now we have amazing memories that will last a lifetime.

> ♥ *"Trust in the Lord with all your heart, and lean not on your own understanding; in all your ways acknowledge Him, and He shall direct your paths".*
>
> (Proverbs 3:5-6).

A Church in a Garbage Dump

Visiting Mexico in 2009 was not on my calendar of things to do. My focus was to finish this book and stay focused on getting it published. However, the Lord had other plans—I ended up ministering in Mexico three times that year. I've learned not to question, but to be obedient when the call of God tells you to *go*.

Before I left on this medical mission trip to Mexico City, many in the community asked, "Jan, when the economy is so bad,

SHE DARES TO *Dream*

Children playing in a garbage dump outside of Mexico City

and there are dangers of earthquakes, violence, and the flu, why would you get on a plane and go to a place where you don't know the language, the people don't know you, and you may never see them again?"

My answer is: I knew I was *called* to go. I believe that the God who calmed the stormy sea is the same God who would calm my heart through any storms that might come my way. And the storms did come—a hailstorm the day we arrived, a sprained ankle the day after my arrival, and a lost tire on our bus as we were driving to the garbage dump. However, all that the enemy tried to do to discourage us didn't matter. Our small team from Hillcrest Church was powerful and was determined to minister regardless of the circumstances.

Partnering with Operation Serve International was the best. They were well organized and with their help, we provided medical, dental, and optical services to some very poor people.

Because of my sprained ankle, I served as a pointer in the optical area. It was incredible seeing children, teenagers, adults, and the elderly being fitted for glasses—many for the first time in their lives. After many attempts to find just the correct formula, they were handed a pair of eyeglasses and some read the Bible for the first time. As we ministered and prayed with the patients, many accepted Jesus into their lives.

Arriving at the garbage dump was an experience I will never forget. Tears came to my eyes as I watched the children smiling and playing like nothing was wrong. Their entire playground consisted of one swing on a metal structure. I have seen much poverty in my life, but nothing quite like this. The amazing Green

Wow Stories

family from Hillcrest Church, with their three young children, were a breath of fresh air to these people. They provided face painting, nail coloring, and clowning—an amusement seldom experienced by these youngsters.

Walking through a clearing to a small tin bathroom, we came upon a tiny one-room wooden chapel in the midst of the dump. Beams of light streamed through the cracks in the small dark room as our team praised God and prayed for miracles in this humble place. It touched me to realize that these people took the little they had and built a chapel for the poorest of the poor. I would love to have been there on a Sunday to attend a service.

Another day, we visited a village church and heard the pastor remark, "I've been praying for years for a team like this to come and serve my people." I couldn't help but think of how blessed we are in America to have such marvelous settings to honor God. The food cooked by church members to say "thank you" to our team, when they had so little themselves, was like Jesus saying, *I'm so pleased you were willing to go and be My hands and feet.*

I am always grateful for those who were generous enough to *send* me. Please remember that it is never too late to go out on the mission field. You will find it to be one of the most meaningful experiences of your life, whatever your age. Many will be grateful that you came.

> ♥ *"How beautiful on the mountains are the feet of those who bring good news, who proclaim peace, who bring good tidings, who proclaim salvation..."*
> (Isaiah 52:7 NIV).

Part Four

Leave A Living Legacy

*Bill Tennyson, daughter Lisa, son James,
Granddaughter Madeline, Jan Tennyson, grandson Robby,
daughter-in-law Dana,
Twin grandchildren, Lane and Samantha
2007*

Chapter Thirteen

The Best is Yet to Come

Amazing Grace

God's principles and promises were a secret to me most of my life, because I didn't read the Bible. I was spiritually dry and had no idea about how to forgive those who had wounded me. However, a few years after my divorce from Bill, my life was transformed when I invited Jesus to live in my heart. I wanted to grow spiritually, so I forced myself to open the Bible and spend time in His Word. Through a lot of prayer, I have been able to put the past behind and forgive those who have hurt me. I also have learned that forgiveness does not guarantee reconciliation; but it is a great start.

In spite of our divorce, I was able to reach out to Bill before and after his triple bypass heart surgery in February 2008. As I stood alone at his bedside in the recovery room, there was a special peace in my heart as I gently stroked his forehead, remembering our first date at the Oak Beach Inn at Jones Beach—with my hair blowing in the wind and feeling as free as a bird. That warm memory reminded me of some of the good times we spent together so long ago.

In May 2008, Bill was diagnosed with another shocking report—third stage colon cancer. I continued to pray for a miracle, and at a Sunday morning service at Hillcrest Church in Dallas, Pastor Mark Brand preached—"God can do in a heartbeat what we can't do in a lifetime." His message gave me comfort to know that all would be well. In August 2009, the miraculous report from the doctor stated that Bill was cancer free!

Divorce is never a pretty picture; however, when our motives are pure in keeping relationships alive for the good of a family, with God's help, we can do it.

My friend Mary Dunham Faulkner gives this meaningful advice in her book, *Gentle Wisdom for Tough Times*:

> *"A good reason to love long and forgive quickly is because you never know when you will need that person to help see you through the tough times. Not one of us can make it on our own. We need each other, especially our own family. Families who work to stay close together during the difficult storms of life make it for the long haul and are still together to celebrate the joyous times. And you can be sure they will come…you just have to wait for them."*

The Power of the Written Word

Most of my life, I wasn't much of a reader. I can't remember anyone reading to me as a child, or spending time with me at the library. My foster mother demanded that we come straight home from school. We were not allowed to go to the library or anyplace else.

When my children were little, I enrolled them in "story time" at our local library. I wanted them to enjoy reading at an early age. During that hour, I spent my time in the self-help section.

It wasn't until after our divorce that I discovered that the real answers to life's problems were in the Bible. Learning about God's promises changed my life. My mind was open to a whole new way of thinking.

Today, I treasure the wide variety of books in my library at home. It is filled with travel and motivational/inspirational books—many authored by friends who have genuinely impacted my life.

Sipping a cup of herbal tea in my prayer room at home while gazing at the picture of a window that looks out to a white sandy beach is one of my favorite settings to read. I dream that I'm sitting at my cottage by the sea. Reading in this quiet, peaceful, place allows me to grow emotionally and spiritually. As I turn the pages of a book, my imagination takes me to joyful places today and helps create amazing visions of happy tomorrows.

In today's world, it seems that our happy tomorrows are at risk. Technology is wonderful. But when our closest companions are computers, cell phones, texting, iPods, and video games, intimate face-to-face conversations with our families become fewer and shorter.

Today we have a choice to be intentional about communicating face to face. It sometimes means taking a trip that we hadn't planned, but learning what is going on in each other's lives and asking questions about those who came before us is important. By knowing the past, we can change our future.

It seems that family history is being lost because many are not taking the challenge to preserve it. My friend, Helen Hosier, expresses this best in *The Grandmother's Bible* NIV. She notes it as *A Scroll of Remembrance* as mentioned in Malachi 3:16. Helen writes about the connectedness bridge—the link to family history.

"The importance of the family, its roots and ties even to other countries, is kept in remembrance for future generations when we are diligent to assume the responsibility for preserving it."

Unfolding my family history has taken me nearly a lifetime to discover, but the journey was worth it. The record shows that there *was* a Lowery family intact at one time, and the storms that came destroyed much of their lives. That fact is now history—but I believe for my family TODAY—the best is yet to come.

My children enrich my life. They are happily married with children and homes of their own. I am happy because God's amazing grace has allowed our family to spend Christmas, Easter, and birthday celebrations together—grandparents, parents, and grandchildren. I pray that my family will cherish their roots and know that with God, all things can be made beautiful in His time.

♥ *"Be anxious for nothing, but in everything by prayer and supplication, with thanksgiving, let your requests be made known to God. and the peace of God which surpasses all understanding, will guard your hearts and minds through Christ Jesus. "*
(Philippians 4:6 NKJV).

THE BEST IS YET TO COME

SHE DARES TO DREAM

Jan with a student at the White House, Washington, D.C

As I pen these final words of my life story for now, I am excited about what lies ahead. I wonder,

Is this my first and only book? Will I be inspired to write more?

Will my children or grandchildren join me in my quest to inspire the brokenhearted?

Will I speak to audiences in private homes, churches, conference centers, and/or on cruise ships signing books that will inspire people to live their dream?

Will I fly to an exotic island and sit under a palm tree reading all the books on my "to read" list?

Will I have a yacht and go from island to island, gathering with the natives and telling them about the greatest Man who ever lived?

Will I spend time on the Amalfi Coast in Italy, overlooking the Mediterranean, reading my favorite books and introducing people to a heavenly Father?

Will I conduct Dare to Dream banquets in orphanages, on beaches, in boardrooms, in fine restaurants, or in a simple home? ... Only God knows.

I don't have my white wicker rockers on the porch of a home with a veranda filled with flowers overlooking the water that I dreamed about so many years ago. But I believe in the beauty of my dreams—so I dream on....

Over the years I have learned that when God calls you, it doesn't matter if you were born into poverty or didn't have a stable family upbringing. God chooses ordinary people as well as those considered outsiders or social outcasts as His future leaders and ambassadors. In God's eyes, there are no losers.

As I recall my birthday in July 1992 when Mary Kay Ash encouraged me to begin writing this book, I wish that she could be here to watch me cross the finish line. Heaven is not that far away, and I believe she is smiling as I tell people about the heart necklace with the mustard seed that she gave me so long ago. Today, as I think fondly of her, I am reminded of the scripture—

♥ *"Everything is possible for him who believes"*
(Mark 9:23 NIV).

THE BEST IS YET TO COME

This story is not over. A new, exciting chapter of life is about to unfold. My dream is that *you* will light candles in the hearts of hurting people and share your seeds of encouragement and love.

When we enrich the lives of others, someday they will pass the torch to the next generation and our world will be a better place.

I pray a blessing over each person reading this book—that your path is illuminated by the sunshine of His Spirit and that the peace of His presence is with you always.

To God be the Glory!

Addendum

♥ "The Spirit of the Lord God is upon Me, Because the Lord has anointed me to preach good tidings to the poor; He has sent me to heal the brokenhearted, To proclaim liberty to the captives, And the opening of the prison to those who are bound; To proclaim the acceptable year of the Lord, And the day of vengeance of our God; To comfort all who mourn, To console those who mourn in Zion. To give them beauty for ashes, The oil of joy for mourning, The garment of praise for the spirit of heaviness; That they may be called trees of righteousness, The planting of the Lord, that He might be glorified."

(Isaiah 61:1-3).

Testimonials

"I have received rave reviews concerning your presentation. The information you shared as well as the challenge you gave each of us to Dare to Dream was outstanding."

Carolyn Hunt | Association of Legal Administration, Dallas, Texas

"Your inspirational *Dare to Dream* message to our students at our graduation ceremonies was wonderful! It is motivational people like you who inspire greatness and success in others."

Medical Assistants | Coastline Regional Occupational Program, Costa Mesa, California

"Thank you for speaking to our 850 volunteers at the Tutor Appreciation Banquet. You were wonderful, sincere and motivating.

Masie Bross | Director, City Care's Whiz Kids, Oklahoma City, Oklahoma

"We received so much more than we bargained for. Because of your message, there are two hundred people, ages 16 to 60, who have realized just how special and precious they are.

Professional Business Women | Texas Woman's University, Denton, Texas

"The families are grateful that their dreams have become real because of *Dare to Dream*. Thank you for helping us to provide a safe, loving environment for healing lives and restoring families."

Dorothy Moore | President, Reconciliation Outreach, Dallas, Texas

"I commend you on the superb quality of the seminar. Your organization and packaging of instructional materials highlighted your commitment to details and the pursuit of excellence."

Department of the Army | *Junior ROTC Program*
|Dallas, Texas, Independent School District

"I have devoted twenty-five years to working with at-risk youth. It was refreshing to meet someone who has a calling to work with and provide a sense of hope to disadvantaged children."

James Johnson, Superintendent | Central Oklahoma Juvenile Center, State of Oklahoma

The Independent Charities Seal of Excellence was awarded to *Dare to Dream* Children's Foundation as one of the Best in America. The members of Independent Charities of America and Local Independent Charities of America that have, upon rigorous independent review, been able to certify, document, and demonstrate on an annual basis that they meet the highest standards of public accountability, program effectiveness, and cost effectiveness.

These standards include those required by the US Government for inclusion in the Combined Federal Campaign, probably the most exclusive fund drive in the world. Of the 1,000,000 charities operating in the United States today, it is estimated that fewer than 50,000, or 5% meet or exceed these standards, and, of those, fewer than 2,000 have been awarded this seal.

2007 Texas Governor's Lonestar Achievement Award

2007 Ebby Halliday Rose of Distinction Award

2006 Outstanding Woman of Today— Altrusa International, Richardson, Texas

2006 Best in America seal—Local Independent Charities

2003 Faithfulness Award—Texas Youth Commission

2002 Honored at Dallas Community Appreciation Festival—TYC and Dallas Community Advisory Council

2001 Longevity Award—Dallas County Juvenile Department

1998 Furhrman's Group Community Support Award—Texas Youth Commission

1997 Volunteer of the Year Award— Dallas County Juvenile Department

1996 Furhman's Group Service Award— Texas Youth Commission

**24th Annual Governor's Volunteer Awards Winner
Governor's Lonestar Achievement**

*In recognition of your outstanding contributions to the State of Texas
Presented to Jan Tennyson by Governor Rick Perry
November 2007, Austin, Texas.*

Dare to Dream Children's Foundation

Serving wounded youth since 1987

"Dare to Dream is worthy of your support. Our children come from many challenging life situation such as homeless, in financial crisis, facing illness, addictions, and tremendous stress. Dare to Dream volunteers gives the children a chance to rediscover lost smiles."

Larry Mercer | *former Director of Buckner Children's Home and former Advisory Board Member of Dare to Dream.*

To donate or volunteer with *Dare to Dream* Children's Foundation, please visit www.daretodream–dallas.org. An application and an opportunity form may be found in the Volunteer Section.

It is only by the prayers and generosity of people like you that we can sustain our programs and events for abused, neglected and foster children—those who have nowhere else to turn and truly need our help.

Please pray about sending a donation and investing in the lives of wounded teenagers who, with our help, can become productive citizens of tomorrow. Your investment will have eternal value.

May God abundantly bless any seed that you plant into this ministry.

Jan Tennyson,

Founder

A Sincere Thank You

Author Portrait—Kevin Brown Photo

Piano Gallery, Dallas, Texas—Bob Rosenthal, Owner

Part II Portrait of Jan Tennyson—Bob Mader 1987

Painting—"The Invitation" © 2010 DaySpring Cards and Morgan Weistling. Used by permission, all rights reserved. www.dayspring.com

Volunteer Group Photos—Mark Brooks

2007 Tennyson Family Photo - Isaac Photography

Dare to Dream website: www.daretodream-dallas.org by David Russell—Red Spot Design, www.redspotdesign.com

One Solitary Life

There was a man born of Jewish parents in an obscure village. The child of a peasant woman, he grew up in another obscure village.

He worked in a carpenter shop until he was thirty. Then for just three years he was an itinerant preacher.

He never wrote a book. He never held an office. He never owned a home.

He never had a family. He never went to college. He never put his foot inside a big city. He never traveled two hundred miles from the place where He was born.

He never did any of the things that usually accompany greatness. He had no credentials but himself.

While he was still a young man, the tide of popular opinion turned against him. His friends ran away. He was turned over to his enemies. He went through the mockery of a trial.

He was nailed to a cross between two thieves and His executioners gambled for the only piece of property he had on earth—His coat.

When he was dead, he was taken down and was laid in a borrowed grave.

Two thousand years have come and gone and today he is the central figure of the human race.

All the armies that ever marched, and all the navies that ever sailed, and all the parliaments that ever sat, and all the kings that ever reigned, put together, have not affected the life of man upon this earth as powerfully as that *one solitary life*.

Excerpts from writing by James Allen Francis (1864–1928)

She Dares to *Dream*
The Jan Tennyson Story

A wounderful gift for Birthdays, Anniversaries, Holidays, Bon voyage, Road trips, or a special gift to say, "I care."

For additional copies of this book
or to schedule Speaking Engagements

Contact Jan Tennyson

www.daretodream—dallas.org
214-599-9563

Dare to Dream Children's Foundation
6310 LBJ Freeway, Suite 111
Dallas, Texas 75240